بسم الله الرحمن الرحيم

ETERNITY HAS ALREADY BEGUN

HARUN YAHYA

Goodword
B·O·O·K·S

First published 2001
© Goodword Books 2001

Goodword Books
1, Nizamuddin West Market,
New Delhi 110 013
Tel. 435 5454, 435 1128, 435 6666
Fax 435 7333, 435 7980
E-mail: info@goodwordbooks.com
Website: www.goodwordbooks.com

Printed in India

To The Reader

The reason why a special chapter is assigned to the collapse of the theory of evolution is that this theory constitutes the basis of all anti-spiritual philosophies. Since Darwinism rejects the fact of creation, and therefore the existence of God, during the last 140 years it has caused many people to abandon their faith or fall into doubt. Therefore, showing that this theory is a deception is a very important duty, which is strongly related to the religion. It is imperative that this important service be rendered to everyone. Some of our readers may find the chance to read only one of our books. Therefore, we think it appropriate to spare a chapter for a summary of this subject.

In all the books by the author, faith-related issues are explained in the light of the Qur'anic verses and people are invited to learn God's words and to live by them. All the subjects that concern God's verses are explained in such a way as to leave no room for doubt or question marks in the reader's mind. The sincere, plain and fluent style employed ensures that everyone of every age and from every social group can easily understand the books. This effective and lucid narrative makes it possible to read them in a single sitting. Even those who rigorously reject spirituality are influenced by the facts recounted in these books and cannot refute the truthfulness of their contents.

This book and all the other works of the author can be read individually or discussed in a group at a time of conversation. Those readers who are willing to profit from the books will find discussion very useful in the sense that they will be able to relate their own reflections and experiences to one another.

In addition, it will be a great service to the religion to contribute to the presentation and reading of these books, which are written solely for the good pleasure of God. All the books of the author are extremely convincing. For this reason, for those who want to communicate the religion to other people, one of the most effective methods is to encourage them to read these books.

In these books, you will not find, as in some other books, the personal views of the author, explanations based on dubious sources, styles that are unobservant of the respect and reverence due to sacred subjects, nor hopeless, doubt-creating, and pessimistic accounts that create deviations in the heart.

About The Author

The author, who writes under the pen-name HARUN YAHYA, was born in Ankara in 1956. He studied arts at Istanbul's Mimar Sinan University and philosophy at Istanbul University. Since the 1980s, the author has published many books on political, faith-related and scientific issues. Harun Yahya is well-known as an author who has written very important works disclosing the forgery of evolutionists, the invalidity of their claims and the dark liaisons between Darwinism and bloody ideologies.

His pen-name is made up of the names "Harun" (Aaron) and "Yahya" (John), in memory of the two esteemed prophets who fought against lack of faith. The Prophet's seal on the cover of the author's books has a symbolic meaning linked to the their contents. This seal represents the Qur'an as the last Book by God and the last word of Him and our Prophet, the last of all the prophets. Under the guidance of the Qur'an and Sunnah, the author makes it his main goal to disprove each one of the fundamental tenets of disbelieving ideologies and to say the "last word", so as to completely silence the objections raised against religion. The seal of the Prophet, who attained ultimate wisdom and moral perfection, is used as a sign of his intention of saying this last word.

All these works by the author centre around one goal: to convey the message of the Qur'an to people and thus to encourage them to think about basic faith-related issues, such as the existence of God, His unity and the hereafter, and to remind them of some important issues.

Harun Yahya enjoys a wide readership in many countries such as India, America, England, Indonesia, Poland, Bosnia, Spain and Brazil. His books have been translated into many languages, and English, French, German, Italian, Portuguese, Urdu, Arabic, Albanian, Russian, Serbo-Croat (Bosnian), Uygur Turkish, and Indonesian versions are available.

Greatly appreciated all around the world, these works have been instrumental in many people putting their faith in God and in many others gaining a deeper insight into their faith. The wisdom, and the sincere and easy-to-understand style employed give these books a distinct touch which directly strikes any one who reads or examines them. Immune to objections, these works are characterised by their features of rapid effectiveness, definite results and irrefutability. The explanations provided in the books are undeniable, explicit and sincere, and enrich the reader with definitive answers. It is unlikely that those who read these books and give a serious thought to them can any longer sincerely advocate the materialistic philosophy, atheism and any other perverted ideology or philosophy. Even if they continue to advocate, this proves to be only a sentimental insistence since these books refute these ideologies from their very basis. All contemporary movements of denial are ideologically defeated today, thanks to the collection of books written by Harun Yahya.

There is no doubt that these features result from the wisdom and lucidity endowed them by God. The author certainly does not feel proud of himself; he merely intends to serve as a means in one's search for God's right path. Furthermore, the author makes no material gains from his books. Neither the writer, nor those who are instrumental in publishing and making these books accessible to the reader, make any material gains. They merely serve to earn the good pleasure of God.

Considering these facts, those who encourage people to read these books, which open the "eyes" of the heart and guide them in becoming more devoted servants of God, render an invaluable service.

Meanwhile, it would just be a waste of time and energy to propagate books which create confusion in people's minds, lead people into ideological chaos, and which clearly have no strong and precise effects in removing the doubts in peoples' hearts. It is apparent that it is impossible for books devised to put the stress on author's literary power rather than the noble goal of saving people from loss of faith, to have such a great effect. Those who doubt this can readily see that the sole aim of Harun Yahya's books is to overcome disbelief and to disseminate the moral values of the Qur'an. The success, impact and sincerity this service has rendered are manifest in the reader's conviction.

One point needs to be kept in mind: The main reason for the continuing cruelty and conflict, and all the ordeals Muslims undergo is the ideological prevalence of lack of religion. These things can only come to an end with the ideological defeat of lack of faith and by ensuring that everybody knows about the wonders of creation and Qur'anic morality, so that people can live by it. Considering the state of the world today, which forces people into the downward spiral of violence, corruption and conflict, it is clear that this service has to be provided more speedily and effectively. Otherwise, it may be too late.

It is no exaggeration to say that the Harun Yahya series have assumed this leading role. By the Will of God, these books will be the means through which people in the 21st century will attain the peace and bliss, justice and happiness promised in the Qur'an.

The works of the author include The Disasters Darwinism Brought to Humanity, Communism in Ambush, The 'Secret Hand' in Bosnia, The Holocaust Hoax, Behind the Scenes of Terrorism, Israel's Kurdish Card, Solution: The Morals of the Qur'an, The Evolution Deceit, Perished Nations, For Men of Understanding, The Prophet Musa, The Golden Age, Allah's Artistry in Colour, Glory is Everywhere, The Truth of the Life of This World, Knowing the Truth, The Dark Magic of Darwinism, The Religion of Darwinism, The Qur'an Leads the Way to Science, The Real Origin of Life, The Consciousness of the Cell, The Creation of the Universe, Miracles of the Qur'an, The Design in Nature, Self-Sacrifice and Intelligent Behaviour Models in Animals, Children Darwin Was Lying!, The End of Darwinism, Deep Thinking, Never Plead Ignorance.

The author's other works on Quranic topics include: Devoted to Allah, Abandoning the Society of Ignorance, Paradise, Knowledge of the Qur'an, Qur'an Index, Emigrating for the Cause of Allah, The Character of Hypocrites in the Qur'an, The Secrets of the Hypocrite, The Names of Allah, Communicating the Message and Disputing in the Qur'an, Answers from the Qur'an, Death Resurrection Hell, The Struggle of the Messengers, The Avowed Enemy of Man: Satan, Idolatry, The Religion of the Ignorant, The Arrogance of Satan, Prayer in the Qur'an, The Importance of Conscience in the Qur'an, The Day of Resurrection, Never Forget, Disregarded Judgements of the Qur'an, Human Characters in the Society of Ignorance, The Importance of Patience in the Qur'an, General Information from the Qur'an, The Mature Faith, Before You Regret, Our Messengers Say, The Mercy of Believers, The Fear of Allah, The Nightmare of Disbelief, Prophet Isa Will Come, Beauties Presented by the Qur'an for Life, Bouquet of the Beauties of Allah 1-2-3-4, The Iniquity Called "Mockery", The Secret of the Test, The True Wisdom According to the Qur'an, The Struggle with the Religion of Irreligion, The School of Yusuf, The Alliance of the Good, Slanders Spread Against Muslims Throughout History, The Importance of Following the Good Word, Why Do You Deceive Yourself?, Islam: The Religion of Ease, Enthusiasm and Vigor in the Qur'an, Seeing Good in Everything, How does the Unwise Interpret the Qur'an?, Some Secrets of the Qur'an, The Courage of Believers, Being Hopeful in the Qur'an, Justice and Tolerance in the Qur'an

Contents

Introduction

*W*hat does the word "eternity" mean to you?

One always tends to associate the concept of eternity with figures such as a thousand years, one million or a billion years. Such a concept of time seems to suggest an everlasting period. Similarly, what the concept of "infinite distance" evokes in the mind is great distances, like a hundred thousand or a million light years.

Nevertheless, even if you endeavour to think of the greatest figure possible, you are still limited by the intellectual capacity of your mind. An example would contribute to a fuller understanding of the extraordinary extent of **eternity**: if a quadrillion of people spent all their lives, lasting also a quadrillion years, doing nothing but counting numbers, day and night without stopping, they would still fail to arrive at eternity, since eternity as a concept has no beginning and no end.

However, in the sight of God, the Almighty, this concept of the "everlasting" and accordingly absolutely incomputable, has already ended. Eternity, which appears to be an unattainable concept for us, is actually **just a single moment in the sight of God.**

This book presents to you unprecedented explanations of timelessness, spacelessness and eternity, and makes you confront an important fact: that eternity has already begun. The realization of this fact will make you once again appreciate God, the Almighty and Exalted, and His creation. Meanwhile, you will find comprehensible answers to some frequently asked questions: Where is God? What is the resurrection? What is the true nature of death? Is there an endless life? and When will all these happen?

Yet, before proceeding with these issues, some concepts like "the real nature of matter" and "timelessness," will be dealt with in detail for a better comprehension of the above-mentioned subject.

The Secret Beyond Matter

WARNING

The chapter you are about to read reveals CRUCIAL SECRETS of your life. You should read it very attentively and thoroughly, for it concerns a subject that is liable to make fundamental changes in your outlook on the external world, the concept of time, and eternity. The subject of this chapter is not just a point of view, a different approach, or a traditional or philosophical thought: it is a fact which everyone, believing or unbelieving, will admit and which is also proven by science today..

*T*he concept of "the nature of matter" is one liable to change one's outlook on life, and indeed, one's whole life, once its essence is known. This subject is directly related to the meaning of your life, your expectations from the future, your ideals, passions, desires, plans, the concepts you esteem, and the material things you possess.

The subject matter of this chapter, "the nature of matter", is not a subject raised today for the first time. Throughout the history of humanity, many thinkers and scientists have discussed this concept. Right from the start, people have been divided into two groups on this issue; one group, known as materialists, based their philosophies and lives on the substantial existence of matter and lived by deceiving themselves. Another group acted sincerely, and being unafraid of thinking more profoundly, led their lives by grasping the essence of the "things" to which they were exposed and the deep meaning lying beyond them. However, advances in the science and technology of our age have finally ended this controversy by indisputably proving the self-evident fact that matter has no substantial existence.

The importance of the subject comes from its impact on man's whole life. Every person has a limited lifetime, and everyone is tested by God during this period. Each individual will subsequently be recompensed strictly according to the path he chose to follow, the manners and character he displayed in this world, his eternal life being shaped by what he has merited. This means that in his endless life, he will be requited for the life he has chosen in the world, and will never again have the chance to make amends for his mistakes.

From this viewpoint, it is easier to understand the value of people's lives on earth. Hence the importance of the subject tackled in this book. Since everyone has a short test time, and will be rewarded or punished for his deeds in his endless afterlife, then it surely follows that he must spend this period in the wisest way. If he fails to do that, his ultimate remorse will be of no avail.

The purpose of this book is to help man before he reaches the stage of repentance, with no chance of atonement on "that day" when man will go to his Creator **"all alone just as He created him at first."** (Surat al-An'am: 94)

The real nature of matter is first addressed, therefore, from a scientific perspective. As we have earlier stated, the subjects described here are definitely not a matter of opinion or a philosophical idea, but facts proved in many fields of science. However, this subject is not a complex, incomprehensible or difficult one, as is commonly supposed. Anyone who does not flinch from thinking and who sincerely reflects upon reality will easily come to a very important conclusion in terms of his own life, once he has grasped these facts.

What you will read now will perhaps become the key to many issues which you were hitherto unable to resolve or completely understand; you will have a fuller comprehension of concepts such as paradise, hell, and the hereafter in depth and live by acknowledging the meaning of life.

The Long Discussed Question: What is the Real Nature of Matter?

Someone who conscientiously and wisely contemplates the universe he inhabits, the galaxies, the planets, the balance therein, the willpower in the structure of the atom, the order he comes across in every part of the universe, the countless living species around him, the way they live, their amazing traits, and finally his own body, will instantly realize that there is something extraordinary about all these things. He will readily understand that this perfect order and the subtleties around him could not have originated by themselves, but must certainly have had a Creator.

The question we must answer is: "By Whom were all these things created?"

It is obvious that **"the fact of creation,"** which is self-evident in every domain of the universe, cannot be an outcome of the universe itself. For example, a peacock, with its colouring and design implying a matchless art, cannot have created itself. The miniscule equilibriums in the universe cannot have created or organized themselves. Neither plants, humans, bacteria, erythrocytes (red-blood corpuscles), nor butterflies can have created themselves. Moreover, the possibility that all these entities could have originated "by chance" is not even imaginable.

It is evident that everything that we see has been created, but none of the things we see can themselves be "creators." The Creator is different from and superior to all that we see with our eyes. He is invisible, but everything He has created reveals His existence and attributes.

This is the point at which those who deny the existence of God demur. Such people have been conditioned not to believe in His existence unless they see Him with their eyes. In their view, there is a heap of matter throughout the whole universe, spreading out until eternity and God is nowhere in this heap of matter. Even if they travelled thousands of light years, they think they would not meet God. This is why they deny His existence. Therefore, these people, who disregard the fact of **"creation,"** are forced to reject the actuality of "creation" manifest throughout the universe and try to prove that the universe and the living things in it have not been created. However, it is impossible for them to do this, because every corner of the universe overflows with the evidence of God's being.

The basic mistake of those who deny God is shared by many people who do not really deny the existence of God but have a wrong perception of Him. They do not deny the signs of "creation" which are everywhere manifest but have superstitious beliefs about **"where" God is**. Most of them think that God is up in the "sky." They tacitly and wrongly imagine that God is behind a very distant planet and interferes with "worldly" affairs" once in a while, or perhaps does not intervene at all. They imagine that He created the universe and then left it to itself, leaving people to determine their fates for themselves.

Still others have heard the fact stated in the Qur'an that God is "everywhere," but they cannot conceive of what exactly this means. In accordance with the distorted thought in their subconscious, they think that God surrounds everything—like radio waves or like an invisible, intangible gas.

However, this and other beliefs that are unclear about **"where" God is** (and maybe because of that deny Him) are all based on a common mistake. They are prejudiced without reason and so are liable to have wrong opinions of God. What is this prejudice?

This prejudice is about the nature and characteristics of matter. Man is so conditioned in his suppositions about the existence of matter that he never thinks about whether it does or does not exist, or whether it is only a shadow. Modern science demolishes this prejudice and discloses a very important and revealing reality. In the following pages, we will clarify this great reality to which the Qur'an points.

We Live in a Universe Presented to Us by Our Perceptions

According to Albert Camus, you can grasp and count happenings through science, but you cannot grasp the universe. Here is the tree, you feel its hardness; here is the water, you taste it. Here is the wind, it cools you. You have to be satisfied with all that.[1] All the information that we have about the realness of the world in which we live is conveyed to us by our five senses. The world we know of consists of what our eyes see, our hands feel, our noses smell, our tongues taste, and our ears hear. We never think that the "external" world could be anything other than that which our senses present to us, as we have been dependent solely on those senses since birth.

Modern research in many different fields of science points to a very different fact and creates serious doubt about our senses and the world that we perceive with them.

According to scientific findings, **what we perceive as "the external world," is only the result of the brain being stimulated by the electrical signals sent to it by our sense organs.** The multi-hued colours you perceive with your sense of sight, the feeling of hardness or softness conveyed by your sense of touch, the tastes you experience on your tongue, the different notes and sounds you hear with your ear, the variety of scents you smell, your work, your home, all your possessions, the lines of this book, and moreover, your mother, your father, your family, the whole world you have always seen, known, got used to throughout your life, are **comprised purely and simply of electrical signals sent by your sense organs to the brain.** Though this seems difficult on the first analysis, this is a scientific fact. The views of renowned philosophers like Bertrand Russell and L. Wittgeinstein on this subject are as follows:

> For instance, whether a lemon truly exists or not and how it came to exist cannot be questioned or investigated. A lemon consists merely of a taste sensed by the tongue, an odour sensed by the nose, a colour and shape sensed by the eye; and only these features of it can be subject to examination and assessment. Science can never know the physical world.[2]

Frederick Vester explains the point that science has reached on this subject:

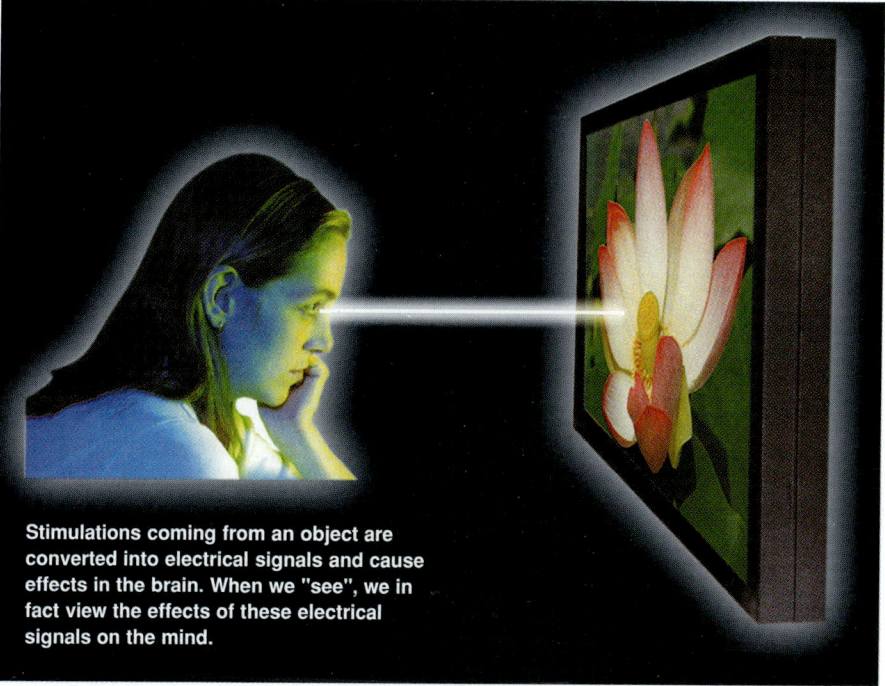

Stimulations coming from an object are converted into electrical signals and cause effects in the brain. When we "see", we in fact view the effects of these electrical signals on the mind.

The statements of certain scientists that "man is an image, everything experienced is temporary and deceptive, and this universe is a shadow," seem to be proven by science in our day. [3]

The thoughts of the famous philosopher, George Berkeley, on the subject can be summarised like this:

> We believe in the existence of objects just because we see and touch them, and they are reflected to us by our perceptions. However, our perceptions are only ideas in our mind. Thus, objects we captivate by perceptions are nothing but ideas, and these ideas are essentially in nowhere but our mind... Since all these exist only in the mind, then it means that we are beguiled by deceptions when we imagine the universe and things to have an existence outside the mind. So, none of the surrounding things have an existence out of our mind. [4]

In order to clarify the subject, let us consider our sense of sight, which provides us with the most extensive information about the external world.

How Do Our Sense Organs Work?

Few people think deeply on how the act of seeing takes place. Everyone answers the question "How do we see?" by saying "with our eyes for sure." However, when we look at the technical explanation of the process of seeing, it seems that that is not the case. The act of seeing is realized progressively. Light clusters (photons) travel from the object to the eye and pass through the lens at the front of the eye where they are refracted and fall upside down on the retina at the back of the eye. Here, impinging light is turned into electrical signals that are transmitted by neurons to a tiny spot called the centre of vision in the back of the brain. The act of seeing actually takes place in this tiny spot in the posterior part of the brain, which is **pitch-dark and completely insulated from light.**

Now, let us reconsider this seemingly ordinary and unremarkable process. When we say, "we see," we are, in fact, seeing the effects of impulses reaching our eyes and induced in our brain, after they are transformed into electrical signals. That is, when we say, "we see," **we are actu-**

ally observing the aggregate of the electrical signals in our mind. There-fore, seeing is not a process terminating in the eye; our eye is only a sense organ serving as a means in the process of seeing.

All the images we view in our lives are formed in our centre of vision, in the size of a nut, which only comprises a few cubic centimetres of the volume of the brain. Both the book you are now reading, and the screen of your computer, and the boundless landscape you see when you gaze at the horizon, and the seamless sea, and a crowd of people who participate in a marathon, fit into this tiny space. Another point that has to be kept in mind is that, as we have noted before, **the brain is insulated from light;** its inside is absolutely dark. The brain has no contact with light itself. The place called the centre of vision is a place which is pitch-dark, where light never reaches, so dark that maybe you have never been somewhere like it before. However, you watch a bright, multi-coloured world in this complete darkness. A multi-coloured nature, a glowing landscape, all tones of green, the colours of fruits, the patterns on flowers, the brightness of the sun, all the people in a crowded street, vehicles moving fast in the traffic, hundreds of clothes in a shopping mall, and everything else are all images formed in this pitch dark place. Even the formation of colours in this darkness has still not been discovered. Klaus Budzinski comments:

> ... Chromatists cannot answer the question of how the network in the eye that perceives light as well as colours transmits this information to the brain through sight nerves and what kind of physical-physiological stimulations this creates in the brain.[5]

We can explain this interesting situation with an example. Let us suppose that in front of us there is a burning candle. We can sit opposite this candle and watch it at length. However, during this period, our brain never has any direct contact with the original light of the candle. Even as we feel the heat and light of the candle, the inside of our brain is completely dark and its temperature never changes. We watch a colourful and bright world inside our dark brain.

The same is true of sunlight. Your eye's being dazzled in sunlight or your feeling the scorching heat on your skin does not change the fact that

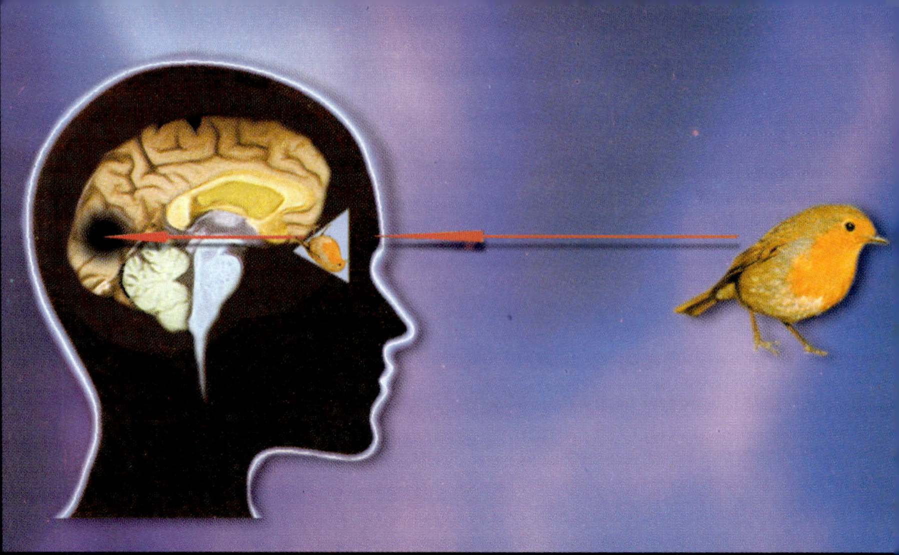

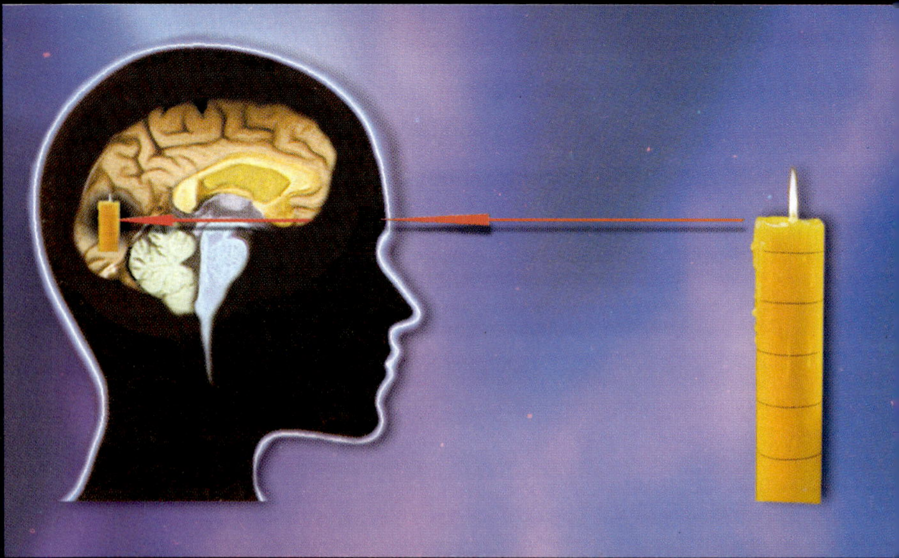

Rays of light coming from an object fall upside-down on the retina as seen in the above picture. Here, the image is converted into electrical signals and transmitted to the centre of vision at the back of the brain. The centre of vision is a very tiny place. Since the brain is insulated from light, it is impossible for light to reach the centre of vision. This means that we view a vast world of light and depth in a tiny spot that is insulated from light. Even at the moment when we feel the light and heat of a fire, the inside of our brain is pitch dark and its temperature never changes.

these are mere perceptions and the centre of vision in your brain is completely dark.

R. L. Gregory gives the following explanation about the miraculous aspects of seeing — something that we take so much for granted:

> We are so familiar with seeing, that it takes a leap of imagination to realize that there are problems to be solved. But consider it. We are given tiny distorted upside-down images in the eyes, and we see separate solid objects in surrounding space. From the patterns of simulation on the retinas we perceive the world of objects, and **this is nothing short of a miracle.**[6]

The same situation applies to all our other senses. Sound, touch, taste, and smell are all perceived as electrical signals in the brain.

The sense of hearing works in a similar manner to that of sight. The outer ear picks up sounds by the auricle and directs them to the middle ear. The middle ear transmits the sound vibrations to the inner ear and intensifies them. The inner ear translates the vibrations into electrical signals, which it sends into the brain. Just as with the eye, the act of hearing finally takes place in the centre of hearing in the brain.

What is true of the eye is also true of the ear, that is, the brain is insulated from sound just as it is from light. Therefore, no matter how noisy it is outside, the inside of the brain is completely silent. Nevertheless, even the subtlest sounds are perceived in the brain. This process is so precise that the ear of a healthy person hears everything without any atmospheric noise or interference. In your brain, which is insulated from sound, and where there is dead silence, you listen to the symphonies of an orchestra, hear all the noises of a crowded place, and perceive all the sounds within a wide frequency range, from the rustling of a leaf to the roar of a jet plane. However, if the sound level in your brain were to be measured by a sensitive device at that moment, it would be seen that complete silence prevailed within it.

Our perception of odour works in a similar way. Volatile molecules emitted by things such as vanilla or a rose reach the receptors in the delicate hairs in the epithelial region of the nose and become involved in an interaction. This interaction is transmitted to the brain as electrical signals and perceived as smell. Everything that we smell, be it pleasant or unpleasant, is nothing but the brain's perception of the interactions of volatile molecules after they have been transformed into electrical signals. You perceive the scent of a perfume, a flower, a food that you like, the sea, or other odours you like or dislike, in your brain. The molecules themselves never reaches the brain. Just as with sound and vision, what reaches your brain as you sense an odour is simply a set of electrical signals. In other words, all the odours that you have assumed – since you were born – to belong to external objects are just electrical signals that you experience through your sense organs. Berkeley also said:

> At the beginning, it was believed that **colours, odours,** etc., "really exist," but subsequently such views were renounced, and it was seen that **they only exist in dependence on our sensations.**[7]

Similarly, there are four different types of chemical receptors in the front part of a human being's tongue. These pertain to the four tastes: salty, sweet, sour, and bitter. Our taste receptors transform these perceptions into electrical signals through a chain of chemical processes and transmit them to the brain. These signals are perceived as taste by the brain. The taste you experience when you eat a chocolate bar or a fruit that you like is the interpretation of electrical signals by the brain. You can never reach the object in the external world; you can never see, smell or taste the chocolate itself. For instance, if the taste nerves that travel to the brain were cut, the taste of things you ate would not reach your brain; you would completely lose your sense of taste.

At this point, we come across another fact:

We can never be sure that what we experience when we taste a food and what another person experiences when he tastes the same food, or what we perceive when we hear a voice and what another person perceives when he hears the same voice are the same. Lincoln Barnett says that **no one can know whether another person perceives the colour red or hears the note C in same way as does he himself.**[8]

We only know as much as our sense organs relate to us. It is impossible for us to reach the physical reality outside us directly. It is again the brain that interprets it. We can never reach the original. Therefore, even when we talk about the same thing, others' brains may be perceiving something different. The reason for this is that what is perceived depends on the perceiver.

The same logic applies to our sense of touch. When we touch an object, all information that will help us recognize the external world and the objects in it is transmitted to the brain by the sense nerves on the skin. The feeling of touch is formed in our brain. Contrary to general belief, the place where we perceive the sense of touch is not at our fingertips, or on our skins, but at the centre of touch perception in our brains. Because of the brain's interpretation of the electrical stimuli coming to it from objects, we experience those objects differently, e.g. they may be hard or soft, hot or cold. We derive all the details that help us recognize an object from these stimuli. The renowned philosopher Bertrand Russell comments in relation to this:

> As to the sense of touch when we press the table with our fingers, that is an electric disturbance on the electrons and protons of our fingertips, produced, according to modern physics, by the proximity of the electrons and protons in the table. **If the same disturbance in our finger-tips arose in any other way, we should have the sensations, in spite of there being no table.**[9]

That the outside world can be identified completely through the senses is a scientific fact. In his book, *A Treatise Concerning the Principles of Human Knowledge*, George Berkeley comments as follows:

> By sight I have the ideas of light and colours, with their several degrees and variations. By touch I perceive hard and soft, heat and cold, motion and resistance. . . . Smelling furnishes me with odours; the palate with tastes; and hearing conveys sounds. . . . And as several of these are observed to accompany each other, they come to be marked by one name, and so to be reputed as one thing. Thus, for example, **a certain colour, taste, smell, figure and consistence having been observed to go together, are accounted one distinct thing, signified by the name apple;** other collections of ideas constitute a stone, a tree, a book, and the like sensible things. . .[10]

Therefore, by processing the data in the centres of vision, sound, smell, taste and touch, our brains, throughout our lives, do not confront the "original" of the matter existing outside us but rather the copy formed inside our brain. It is at this point that we are misled by assuming these copies are instances of the real matter outside us. However, as seen throughout the book, there are also thinkers and scientists who have not been misled by such a misconception, and who have realized this fact.

Even Ali Demirsoy, one of the most famous Turkish materialists, also confessed this truth:

> **In truth, there is neither light as we see it, nor sound as we hear it, nor heat as we sense it in the universe.** Our sense organs mislead us between the external world and brain and give rise to interpretations which are irrelevant to reality in the brain.[11]

Do We Spend Our Entire Life in Our Brains?

From the physical facts described so far, we may conclude the following. Everything we see, touch, hear, and perceive as "matter," "the world" or "the universe" is only electrical signals occurring in our brain. Therefore, someone drinking an orange juice does not confront the actual drink but its perception in the brain. The object considered by the onlooker to be a "drink" actually consists of electrical impressions of the orange colour, sweet taste, and liquid feeling of the orange juice in the brain. The situation is no different while eating chocolate; the electrical data pertaining to the shape, taste, odour, and hardness of the chocolate are perceived in the brain. If the sight nerves travelling to the brain were suddenly to be severed, the image of the chocolate would just as suddenly disappear. A disconnection in the nerve travelling from the sensors in the nose to the brain would completely interrupt the sense of smell.

Put simply, the tree that you see, the objects you smell, the chocolate you taste, and the orange juice you drink are nothing but the brain's interpretation of electrical signals.

Another point to be considered, which might be deceptive, is **the sense of distance.** For example, the distance between you and this book

All we see in our lives is formed in a part of our brain called the "centre of vision" which lies at the back of our brain, and occupies only a few cubic centimetres. Both the image of a small room and the boundless landscape you see when you gaze at the horizon fit into this tiny space. Therefore, we see objects not in their actual sizes existing outside, but in the sizes perceived by our brain.

is only a feeling of space formed in your brain. Objects that seem to be distant from the human viewpoint also exist only in the brain. For instance, someone who watches the stars in the sky assumes that they are millions of light-years away from him. Yet, what he "sees" are really the stars inside himself, in his centre of vision. During a trip, one looks at the city below from a plane and thinks that it is kilometres away from him. However, the whole length and breadth of the city are inside one's brain along with all the people in it.

Today, all scientific data prove that the image we perceive is formed in our brain.

There is yet another misleading, but very important factor. While you read these lines, you are, in truth, not inside the room you assume yourself to be in; on the contrary, the room is inside you. Your seeing your body makes you think that you are inside it. **However, you must remember that your body, too, is an image formed inside your brain.** Bertrand Russell states the following on the subject:

What we can say, on the basis of physics itself, is that what we have hitherto called **our body is really an elaborate scientific construction not corresponding to any physical reality.** [12]

The truth is very clear. If we can feel the external world only through our sense organs, then there would be no consistent reason for us to consider our body to be separate from the external world, that is, to concede that our body has a separate existence.

Our body is also presented to us by the electrical stimulations (impulses) reaching our brain. These impulses, just like all others, are converted into certain sensations, or feelings in our brain. For instance, the feeling of touch occurring when we touch our body with our hand, the feeling of weight caused by the force of gravity, the feeling of seeing caused by the light rays reflected from our body, etc... all these are assessed as a "collection of feelings" by the brain, and we "feel" our body. As revealed by these scientific facts, throughout our lives, we are exposed not to our original body, but to the impulses reaching our brain pertaining to our body. These impulses are identified as "our body" in our perception.

The same applies to all your other perceptions. For instance, when you think that you hear the sound of the television in the next room, you are actually experiencing the sound inside your brain. You can prove neither that a room exists next to yours, nor that a sound comes from the television in that room. Both the sound you think to be coming from metres away and the conversation of a person right next to you are perceived in a centre of hearing in your brain which is only a few square centimetres in size. Apart from within this centre of perception, no concept such as right, left, front or behind exists. That is, sound does not come to you from the right, from the left or from the air; **there is no direction from which sound comes.**

The smells that you perceive are like that too; none of them reaches you from a great distance. You suppose that the end-effects formed in your centre of smell are the smell of the objects in the external world. However, just as the image of a rose is in your centre of vision, so the smell of the rose is in your centre of smell; there is neither a rose nor an odour pertaining to it in the external world.

The same facts hold true also for heat. One of the foremost philosophers of his age, George Berkeley, clarifies with the following example that senses like coldness and hotness cannot be judged to exist outside the mind:

> **Suppose now one of your hands hot, and the other cold, and that they are both at once put into the same vessel of water, in an intermediate state; will not the water seem cold to one hand, and warm to the other?**[13]

Berkeley is right in his analysis. Had heat or cold been present in the matter itself, both hands would have felt the same thing.

The "external world" presented to us by our perceptions is merely a collection of electrical signals reaching our brains. Throughout our lives, our brains process and interpret these signals and we live without recognizing that we are mistaken in assuming that these are the **original** versions of things existing in the "external world". We are misled because **we can never reach these entities themselves by means of our senses.** This point is extremely important.

Moreover, again our brains interpret and attribute meaning to signals that we assume to be the "external world." For example, let us consider the sense of hearing. Our brains transform the sound waves in the "external world" into a rhythm. That is to say, music is also a perception created by our brains. In the same manner, when we see colours, what reaches our eyes is merely **a set of electrical signals of different wavelengths**. Again our brains transform these signals into colours. **There are no colours in the "external world."** Neither is the lemon yellow, nor is the sky blue, nor are the trees green. They are as they are just because

The findings of modern physics show that the universe is a collection of perceptions. The following question appears on the cover of the well-known American science magazine *New Scientist*, which dealt with this topic in its 30 January 1999 issue: "Beyond Reality: Is the Universe Really a Frolic of Primal Information and Matter Just a Mirage?"

we perceive them to be so. The "external world" depends entirely on the perceiver. Colour blindness is important evidence for this. Even the slightest defect in the retina of the eye causes colour blindness. Some people perceive blue as green, and some red as blue. At this point, it does not matter whether the object externally is coloured or not.

According to the prominent thinker Berkeley:

> If the same things can be red and hot for some and the contrary for others, this means that we are under the influence of misconceptions and that "things" only exist in our brains.[14]

In conclusion, the reason we see objects as coloured is not because they are coloured or because they have an independent material existence outside ourselves. Had colours existed outside us, a deficiency called colour blindness would not have existed. The truth of the matter is rather that all the qualities we ascribe to objects are **inside us and not in the "external world."**

Is the Existence of the "External World" Indispensable?

So far, we have been speaking repeatedly of the existence of a world of perceptions formed in our brains, and making the assertion that we can never actually reach this world. Then, how can we be sure that such a world really exists?

Actually, we cannot. Since each object is only a collection of perceptions and those perceptions exist only in the mind, it is more accurate to say that **the only world that really exists is the world of perceptions.** The only world we know of is the world that exists in our mind: the one that is designed, recorded, and made vivid there; the one, in short, that is created within our mind. This is the only world of which we can be sure.

We can never prove that the perceptions we observe in our brain have material correlates. Those perceptions could conceivably be coming from an "artificial" source.

We can visualize this with such an example:

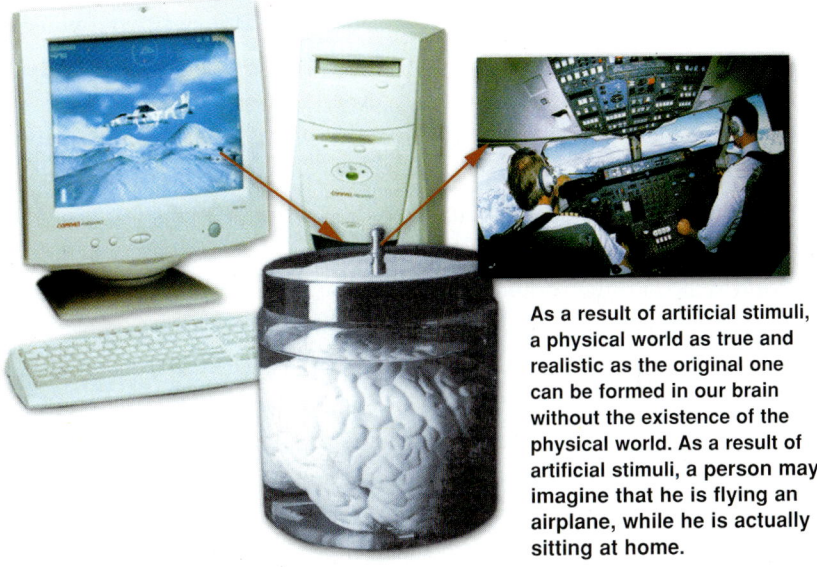

As a result of artificial stimuli, a physical world as true and realistic as the original one can be formed in our brain without the existence of the physical world. As a result of artificial stimuli, a person may imagine that he is flying an airplane, while he is actually sitting at home.

First, let us imagine that we take your brain out of your body and keep it alive artificially in a glass cube. Next to it, let us place a computer with which all kinds of electrical signals can be produced. Then, let us artificially produce and record in this computer the electrical signals of the data related to a setting, such as image, sound, odour, hardness-softness, taste, and body image. This experiment with your brain, which we have taken out of your body, will be carried out on the peak of a deserted mountain. Finally, let us connect the computer to the brain with electrodes that will function as nerves and send the pre-recorded data to your brain which is now high above the clouds. As your brain (which is literally you) perceives these signals, it will see and experience the corresponding setting. For instance, let us suppose that every detail that comes to mind about a football match in a stadium be produced or recorded – in a way to be perceived through the sense organs. In your brain, all by itself at the summit of the mountain, with this recording instrument connected to it, you would feel as if you were living in this artificially created setting. You would think that you were at the match. You would cheer, you would sometimes get angry and sometimes be pleased. Moreover, you would often bump into other people because of the crowd, and therefore feel their existence, too. Most interestingly, everything would be so vivid that you would never doubt the existence of this setting or your body. Or if we sent to your brain the electrical correlates of senses such as seeing, hearing, and touching which you perceive while sitting at a table, your brain would think of itself as a businessman sitting in his office. This imaginary world will continue so long as the stimulations keep coming from the computer. It will never become possible to understand that you consist of nothing but your brain. This is because what is needed to form a world within your brain is not the existence of a real world but rather the stimuli. It is perfectly possible that these stimuli could be coming from an artificial source, such as a recording device or a different kind of perception source. Experiments carried out about this subject demonstrate this fact.

In the U.S.A., Dr. White from Cleveland Hospital, along with his colleagues, all experts in electronics, performed a great feat in making "Cyborg" survive. What Dr. White succeeded in doing was isolating an ape's brain from his skull and feeding it with oxygen and blood. The brain, which was connected to an artificially produced "Heart Lung Machine," was kept alive for five hours. **The device, called an Electro Encephalogram, to which the isolated brain was connected, identified in E.E.G. records that the noises made in the surroundings were heard by this brain and that it reacted to them.**[15]

As we have seen, it is quite possible that we perceive an external world through externally given artificial stimuli. The symbols you would perceive with your five senses are sufficient for this. Other than these symbols, there is nothing left of the external world.

It is indeed very easy for us to be misled into believing perceptions, without any material correlates, to be real. We often experience this feeling in our dreams, in which we experience events, see people, objects and settings that seem completely real. However, they are all, without exception, mere perceptions. There is no basic difference between the "dream" and the "real" world; both of them are experienced in the brain.

Who Is the Perceiver?

As we have related so far, there is no doubt that the world we think we inhabit and know as the "external world" is perceived inside our brain. However, here arises the question of primary importance. Is the will that perceives all these perceptions the brain itself?

When we analyze the brain, we see that it is comprised of lipid and protein molecules, which also exist in other living organisms. As is well known, the essence of these proteins is, in fact, atoms. This means that within the piece of meat we call our "brain," there is nothing to observe the images, to constitute consciousness, or to create the being we call "myself."

R. L. Gregory refers to a mistake people make in relation to the perception of images in the brain:

> There is a temptation, which must be avoided, to say that the eyes produce pictures in the brain. A picture in the brain suggests the need of some kind of internal eye to see it – but this would need a further eye to see its picture... and so on, in an endless regress of eyes and pictures. This is absurd.[16]

This is the very point that puts materialists, who do not hold anything but matter to be true, in a quandary: to whom belongs "the eye inside" that sees, that interprets what it sees and reacts?

Karl Pribram also focused on this important question, about who the perceiver is, in the world of science and philosophy:

> Philosophers since the Greeks have speculated about the "ghost" in the machine, the "little man inside the little man" and so on. Where is the I -- the entity that uses the brain? Who does the actual knowing? Or, as Saint Francis of Assisi once put it, "What we are looking for is what is looking".[17]

Now, think of this: The book in your hand, the room you are in, in brief, all the images in front of you are seen inside your brain. Is it the atoms that see these images? Blind, deaf, unconscious atoms? How would lifeless and unconscious atoms feel, how would they see? Why did some atoms acquire this quality whereas others did not? Do our acts of thinking, comprehending, remembering, being delighted, being unhappy, and everything else consist of the electrochemical reactions between these atoms? No, the brain cannot be the will that performs all of these.

In previous sections, we have pointed out that our body is also included in the collection of perceptions we call the "external world." Therefore, since our brain is also a part of our body, it is also a part of that collection of perceptions. Since the brain itself is a perception, therefore, it cannot be the will that perceives other perceptions.

In his book, *The ABC of Relativity*, Bertrand Russell focuses attention on this subject by saying:

> **Of course, if matter in general is to be interpreted as a group of occurrences, this must apply also to the eye, the optic nerve and the brain.**[18]

It is clear that the being that sees, hears, senses, and feels is a supramaterial being. For matter cannot think, feel, be happy or unhappy. It is not possible to do all these with the body alone. Therefore, this being is neither matter, nor image, but it is "alive." This being relates to the "screen" in front of it by using the image of our body.

An example about dreams will illuminate the subject further. Let us imagine (in accordance with what has been said so far) that we see the dream within our brain. In the dream, we will have an imaginary body, an imaginary arm, an imaginary eye, and an imaginary brain. If during our dream, we were asked, "Where do you see?" we would answer, "I see in my brain." If we were asked where our brain is and what it looks like, we would hold our imaginary head on our imaginary body with our imaginary hand and say, "My brain is a hunk of meat in my head weighing hardly more than a kilo."

Yet, actually there is not any brain to talk about, but an imaginary head and an imaginary brain. The seer of the images is not the imaginary brain in the dream, but a "being" that is far "superior" to it.

We know that there is no physical distinction between the setting of a dream and the setting we call real life. So when we are asked in the setting we call real life the above question: "Where do you see?" it would be just as meaningless to answer "in my brain" as in the example above. In both conditions, the entity that sees and perceives is not the brain, which is after all only a hunk of meat. Realizing this fact, Bergson said in his book, *Matter and Memory*, in summary, that **"the world is made up of images, these images only exist in our consciousness; and the brain is one of these images."**[19]

Therefore, since the brain is a part of the external world, there has to be a will to perceive all these images. **This being is the "soul."**

The aggregate of perceptions we call the "material world" is nothing but a dream observed by this soul. Just as the bodies we possess and the material world we see in our dreams have no reality, the universe we occupy and the bodies we possess also have no material reality. The famous British philosopher David Hume expresses his thoughts on this fact:

> For my part, when I enter most intimately into what I call myself, I always stumble on some particular perception or other, of heat or cold, light or shade, love or hatred, pain or pleasure. I never can catch myself at any time without a perception, and **never can observe any thing but the perception.**[20]

The real being is the soul. Matter consists merely of perceptions viewed by the soul. The intelligent beings that write and read these lines are not each a heap of atoms and molecules and the chemical reactions between them, but a "soul".

The Real Absolute Being

All these facts bring us face to face with a very significant question. If the thing we acknowledge to be the material world is merely comprised of perceptions seen by our soul, then what is the source of these perceptions?

In answering this question, we must consider the following: matter does not have a self-governing existence by itself. Since matter is a perception, it is something "artificial." That is, this perception must have been caused by another power, which means that it must have been created.

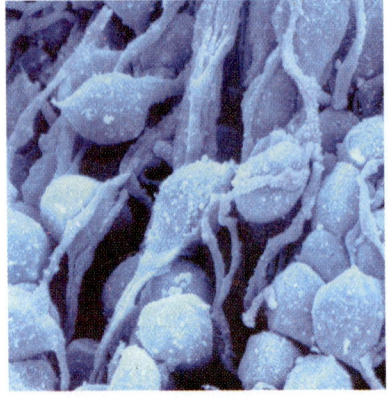

The brain is a collection of cells made up of protein and fat molecules. It is formed of nerve cells called neurons (left). It is certainly not neurons that constitute consciousness. When we examine the structure of neurons, we see atoms. (right) Unquestionably, it is impossible for unconscious atoms to create consciousness. There is no power in this piece of meat to observe images, to constitute consciousness, or to create the being we call "myself".

Moreover, this creation must be continuous. If there were not a continuous and consistent creation, then what we call matter would disappear and be lost. This may be likened to a television screen on which a picture is displayed as long as the signal continues to be broadcast. So, who makes our soul see the stars, the earth, plants, people, our bodies, and all else that we see?

It is very evident that there is a Creator, Who has created the entire material universe, that is, the sum of perceptions, and continues His creation ceaselessly. Since this Creator displays such a magnificent creation, He surely has eternal power and might.

This Creator introduces Himself to us. He sent down a book and through this book has described to us Himself, the universe, and the reason for our existence.

This Creator is God and the name of His book is the Qur'an.

The facts that the heavens and the earth, that is, the universe is not stable, that their presence is only made possible by God's creating them and that they will disappear when He ends this creation, are all explained in a verse as follows:

It is God Who sustains the heavens and the earth, lest they cease (to function): and if they should fail, there is none - not one - can sustain them thereafter: Truly, He is Most Forbearing and Oft-Forgiving. (Surah Fatir: 41)

As we mentioned at the beginning, some people have no genuine understanding of God and so they imagine Him as a being present somewhere in the heavens and not really intervening in worldly affairs. The basis of this logic actually lies in the thought that the universe is an assembly of matter and God is "outside" this material world, in a faraway place. In some false religions, belief in God is limited to this understanding.

However, as we have considered so far, matter is composed only of sensations. And the only real absolute being is God. **That means that only God exists; all things except Him are shadow beings.** Consequently, it is impossible to conceive of God as separate and outside this whole mass of matter. For there is actually nothing such as matter in the sense of being. **God is surely "everywhere" and encompasses all.** This reality is explained in the Qur'an as follows;

God, there is no deity except Him, the Living, the Self-Sustaining. He is not subject to drowsiness or sleep. Everything in the heavens and the earth belongs to Him. Who can intercede with Him except by His permission? He knows what is before them and what is behind them but they cannot grasp any of His knowledge save what He wills. His Footstool encompasses the heavens and the earth and their preservation does not tire Him. He is the Most High, the Magnificent. (Surat al-Baqarah: 255)

That God is not bound by space and that He encompasses everything is stated in another verse as follows:

To God belong the east and the west: Wherever you turn, there is the face of God. For God is all-pervading, all-knowing. (Surat al-Baqarah: 115)

Since material beings are each a perception, they cannot see God; but God sees the matter He created in all its forms. In the Qur'an, this is stated thus: **"No vision can grasp Him, but His grasp is over all vision."** (Surat al-An'am: 103)

That is, we cannot grasp God's being with our eyes, but God has thoroughly encompassed our inside, outside, looks and thoughts. For this reason, God says that **"He controls hearing and sight"** (Surah Yunus: 31). We cannot utter a single word without His knowledge, nor can we even take a breath.

While we watch these sensory perceptions in the course of our lives, the closest being to us is not any one of these sensations, but God Himself. The following verse of the Qur'an asserts this reality: **"It is We Who created man, and We know what dark suggestions his soul makes to him: for We are nearer to him than (his) jugular vein."** (Surah Qaf: 16) When a person thinks that his body is made up only of "matter," he cannot comprehend this important fact. If he takes his brain to be "himself," then the place that he accepts to be the outside is 20-30 cm away from him. According to this reasoning, nothing can be nearer to him than his jugular vein. However, when he understands that there is nothing such as matter, and that everything is imagination, notions such as outside, inside, far or near, lose their meaning. God has encompassed him and He is "infinitely close" to him.

God informs men that He is **"infinitely close"** to them in the verse: **"When My servants ask you about Me, tell them I am indeed close (to them)."** (Surat al-Baqarah: 186). Another verse relates the same fact: **"We have told you that your Lord encompasses all men."** (Surat al-Isra': 60). However, man is misled in thinking that the being closest to him is himself. God, in truth, is even closer to us than ourselves.

He has called our attention to this point in the verse: **"Why is it that when it (the soul) comes up to the throat, and you at that time look on, We are nearer to him than you, but you do not see this."** (Surat al-Waqi'ah: 83-85). Indeed, someone on his death bed, or lying ill can think, although greatly mistaken, that at that moment, the nearest being to him is his doctor beside him, or his mother holding his hand, or one of his dear ones hugging him. However, as also related in the verse, God is nearer to him than everyone else. Yet, people go through life unaware of this phenomenal fact, because they do not see it with their eyes.

The only conclusion to be derived from the sum total of the facts presented here is that the only and real and absolute being is God. With His knowledge, God encompasses man, who is a shadow being, as well as everything else: **"Your god is God alone, there is no god but Him. He encompasses all things in His knowledge."** (Surah Ta Ha: 98). In another verse of the Qur'an, God warns people against such heedlessness:

> **What! Are they in doubt about the meeting with their Lord? What! Does He not encompass all things? (Surah Fussilat: 54)**

Quite the reverse is true of man, who is nothing but a shadow being, and who is so wholly dependent on God, that it is impossible for him to have any independent power or will: **"You will not will unless God wills."** (Surat al-Insan: 39). Another verse showing that everything we experience takes place under God's control runs: **"God has created you and what you do!"** (Surat as-Saffat: 96). In the Qur'an, this reality is stated at many points and with the verse **"You did not throw, when you threw, it was God who threw"** (Surat al-Anfal: 17), it is emphasized that no act is independent of God. Since the human being is a shadow being, he himself does not perform the act of throwing. However, God gives this shadow being the feeling of a "self." In reality, God performs all acts. If someone takes the acts he does as his own, thinks he himself does everything he does, moreover, supposes that he is a being with independent power and puts his trust in this power, he evidently means to deceive himself. For obviously, man is a being totally under the control of God.

This is the reality. The individual may not want to concede this and may think of himself as a being independent of God; but this does not change a thing. Of course his unwise denial is again subject to God's will and desire. In the Qur'an, this fact is addressed thus:

> **It is other than the religion of God that you desire, when everything in the heavens and earth, willingly or unwillingly, submits to Him? To Him you will all be returned. (Surat Al 'Imran: 83)**

God is All-Knowing

God's attribute of "al-Muhit" means "He Who encompasses all." Since God encompasses everything, He is the One Who knows everything people live through. God created all feelings such as pain, soreness, love, pleasure, sadness, and happiness, and therefore God knows all of them very well. Because He knows, He creates and makes His slaves experience them as much as He wills. A point has to be made clear here: God is totally away from these pains and deficiencies. Another attribute of God in the Qur'an is al-Quddus, which means "He Who is unblemished by any error or forgetfulness, and Who is free of imperfection or any kind of defect." All imperfections belong to man.

One of the attributes of God mentioned in the Qur'an is al-Muta'ali, which means "He Who is higher than any action, manner or condition, and any thought that any being may have." This means that God encompasses all things everywhere and knows the innermost secrets of everything. This is "knowing" in the real sense. In order to appreciate the almightiness and omnipotence of God, one needs to have a better grasp of this subject. That God knows the pains, soreness, and every feeling we experience makes us once again understand the fact that God is nearer to us than our jugular vein. God sees man everywhere. Even when he is alone in a sheltered, hidden, secret place, where no one sees him, even when he thinks that he is working at something very secret, God sees him. In the Qur'an, it is stated that God is All-Aware.

> **Do they not know that God knows their secrets and their private talk, and that God is the Knower of all unseen things? (Surat at-Tawbah: 78)**

God hears all words: even at a time when an individual thinks that he is whispering secretly behind barred doors, and solid walls, God hears him. God knows what is in his heart, what he hides from everyone else, as well as those things in his subconscious, of which even he himself is unaware. In the Qur'an, these facts are emphasized:

> **Though you speak out loud, He knows your secrets and what is even more concealed. (Surah Ta Ha: 7)**

Everything That You Possess Is Intrinsically Illusory

As is quite evident, it is a logical, scientific fact that the "external world" has no material reality and that it is a collection of images perpetually presented to our soul by God. Nevertheless, people usually do not include, or rather do not want to include, everything in the concept of the "external world."

Think about this issue sincerely and boldly. You will realize that your house, furniture, car – which has perhaps been recently bought, – office, jewellery, bank account, wardrobe, spouse, children, colleagues, and everything else that you possess are, in fact, included in this imaginary external world projected to you. Everything you see, hear, or smell – in short – perceive with your five senses around you, is a part of this "imaginary world": the voice of your favourite singer, the hardness of the chair you sit on, a perfume whose smell you like, the sun that keeps you warm, a flower with beautiful colours, a bird flying in front of your window, a speedboat moving swiftly on the water, your fertile garden, the computer you use at your job, or your hi-fi that has the most advanced technology in the world...

This is the reality, because the world is only a collection of images created to test man. People are tested all throughout their limited lives with perceptions having no reality. These perceptions are intentionally presented as appealing and attractive. This fact is mentioned in the Qur'an:

> **Fair in the eyes of people is the love of things they covet: Women and sons; heaped-up hoards of gold and silver; horses branded for blood and excellence; and wealth of cattle and well-tilled land. Such are the possessions of this world's life; but in nearness to God is the best of the goals to return to. (Surat Al 'Imran: 14)**

Most people cast their religion away because they have succumbed to the lure of property, wealth, heaped-up hoards of gold and silver, dollars, jewellery, bank accounts, credit cards, wardrobes full of clothes, lat-

If one ponders deeply on all that is said here, one will soon realise this amazing, extraordinary situation by oneself: that all the events in the world are mere imagination...

est-model cars, in short, all the forms of prosperity that they either possess or strive to possess. They concentrate only on this world while forgetting the hereafter. They are deceived by the "fair and alluring" face of the life of this world, and fail to keep up prayer (salat), or give charity to the poor, or perform the kind of worship that will make them prosper in the hereafter. They say instead, "I have things to do," "I have ideals," "I have responsibilities," "I do not have enough time," "I have tasks to complete" or "I will do it later." They consume their lives trying to prosper only in this world. In the verse, **"They know but the outer things in the life of this world: but of the end of things they are heedless"** (Surat ar-Rum: 7), this misconception is defined.

The fact we describe in this chapter, namely, that everything is an image, is very important in that its implications render all lusts and boundaries meaningless. The verification of this fact makes it clear that everything people value, possess or toil to possess – wealth acquired as a result of greed, children of whom they boast, spouses whom they consider closest to them, friends, their own pampered bodies, the social status which they believe to be a form of superiority, the schools they have attended, the holidays on which they have been – is nothing but an illusion. Therefore, all the effort, the time spent, and the satisfaction of greed, prove unavailing.

This is why some people unwittingly make fools of themselves when they boast of their wealth and properties, or of their "yachts, helicopters, factories, holdings, manors, and lands" as if they really existed. Those well-to-do people who ostentatiously sail in their yachts, show off their cars, and keep talking about their wealth, suppose that their posts rank them higher than everyone else, try to make a spectacle of themselves with their dresses, build their entire lives upon such passions and competitions, and keep thinking that they are successful because of all this, should actually think about the state they will find themselves in once they realize that success is nothing but an illusion.

These scenes repeat themselves likewise in dreams. In their dreams, too they have houses, fast cars, extremely precious jewels, rolls of dollars, and loads of gold and silver. In their dreams, they are also positioned in high ranks, own factories with thousands of workers, possess power to rule over many people, and dress in clothes that make everyone admire them. But just as the dreamer would be ridiculed for boasting about the possession he had in his dreams, so would the wide-awake person be equally ridiculed for boasting of the images he sees in this world. For what he sees in his dreams and in this world are both mere images in his mind. Certainly, this fact has to be thought over. As stated in the following verse, those who realize this fact will be successful:

Clear insights have come to you from your Lord. Whoever sees clearly, does so to his own benefit. Whoever is blind, it is to his own detriment. I am not here as your keeper. (Surat al-An'am: 104)

Similarly, the way people react to the events they experience in the world will make them feel ashamed when they realize the reality. Those who fight fiercely with each other, rave furiously, swindle, take bribes, commit forgery, lie, selfishly withhold their money, do wrong to people, beat and curse others, rage aggressively, are full of passion for office and rank, are envious, and show off, will be disgraced when they realize that they have done all of this in a dream world. *So no penalty for action?*

Since God creates all these images, the Ultimate Owner of everything is God alone. This fact is stressed in the Qur'an:

> But to God belong all things in the heavens and on earth: And He it is that encompasses all things. (Surat an-Nisa': 126)

It is great foolishness to cast religion away for the sake of imaginary passions and thus lose the eternal life. Moreover, it will lead one to ever-lasting misfortunes. God predicts the state of the willfully irreligious as follows:

> ...What they achieved here will come to nothing. What they did will prove to be null and void. (Surah Hud: 16) — *? incomplete verse*

As stated in the above verse, both their passions and greed will prove to be null and void, and the things they thought they possessed will be lost in the face of this fact; they will not be of any use, and will become worthless.

At this stage, one point should be understood. It is not maintained here that "the possessions and wealth you have with which you are being stingy, and your children, spouses, friends, and rank will vanish sooner or later, and therefore do not have any meaning," but that "all the possessions you seem to have do not exist; they are merely dreams composed of images which God shows you to test you." As you see, there is a big difference between the two statements. If the former statement were accepted at face value, the individual might be misled into thinking that all these things, people, relationships and worldly status actually existed, albeit temporarily, and he might still work with greed to possess them. But given the latter statement, indicating the true state of affairs, that is, of everything being imaginary, any individual who displayed greed for this purpose would be disgraced and also suffer an unprecedented loss.

Although one does not want to acknowledge this right away and would rather deceive oneself by assuming everything one has truly exists, one is finally to die and in the hereafter everything will be clear when we are recreated. On that day, **"sharp is one's sight"** (Surah Qaf: 22) and we will see everything much more clearly. However, if we have spent our lives chasing after imaginary aims, we are going to wish we had never lived this life and will say: **"Ah! Would that Death had made an end of me! Of no profit to me has been my wealth! And I am bereft of all my power!"** (Surat al-Haqqah: 27-29)

What a wise man should do, on the other hand, is to try to understand the greatest reality of the universe here in this world, while he still has time. Otherwise, he will spend all his life running after dreams and face a grievous penalty at the end. In the Qur'an, the final state of those people who run after illusions (or mirages) in this world and forget their Creator, is stated as follows:

> **As for the unbelievers, their deeds are like a mirage in the sandy desert, which the man parched with thirst mistakes for water; until he comes up to it, and then finds it to be nothing: But he finds God ever with him, and God will pay him back in full: and God is swift in His reckoning.** (Surat an-Nur: 39)

What is the Difference Between the World in Dreams and the World We Perceive Now?

For human beings, reality is all that can be touched with the hand and seen with the eye. Above, we mentioned that our sense organs mislead us and remarked that, scientifically, we can never reach the reality of the external world. The universe of perceptions which we inhabit can be explained also by using the dream analogy. In your dreams, you can also "touch with your hand and see with your eye", but in reality, you have neither hand nor eye, nor is there anything that can be touched or seen. There is no material reality outside your brain that makes these things happen. You are simply being deceived. *in dream only*

What is it that separates real life and dreams from one another? Is it that real life is continuous, and dreams are unconnected, or rather that there are different cause-effect relationships in dreams? Basically, these are not important differences. Ultimately, both forms of living are brought into being within the brain.

If we are able to live easily in an unreal world during our dreams, the same can equally be true for the world we live in while awake. When we wake up from a dream, we can never be sure that we have not entered a longer dream called "real life." The reason we consider our dream a fancy and the world "real" is only a product of our habits and prejudices.

This suggests that we may well be awoken from this life on earth, which we think we are living right now, just as we are awoken from a dream. This point is very important and definitely needs to be reflected upon.

Therefore, it is useful to think about the example of dreams more deeply. A person can experience very realistic events in dream. He can roll down the stairs and break his leg, have a serious car accident, become pinioned under a bus, or eat a cake and be satiated. Similar events to those experienced in our daily lives are also experienced in dreams with the same persuasive sense of their reality, and arousing the same feelings in us. This shows us that perceptions such as taste, touch, or the feeling of hardness can never be evidence of the substantial existence of matter, for these feelings are experienced in dreams with the same sharpness. However, materialists who hold matter to be the absolute being totally fail in understanding this point. In order to prove the existence of matter, they quote examples similar to those above. According to their crooked reasoning, their feeling pain when they give a kick to a stone, or are slapped in the face, their feeling full when they eat a cake, or people's running away seeing a bus on the highway so as not to be knocked down by it are evidence of the existence of matter. The point they fail to understand is that the pain they feel when they give a kick to a stone, the taste they get when they eat a cake, and the perceptions of hardness and physical agony perceived during a bus crash also form in the brain.

A person who dreams that he has been knocked down by a bus can open his eyes in a hospital, again in his dream, and understand that he is disabled, but it is all a dream. He can also dream that he dies in a car crash, angels of death take his soul, and his life in the hereafter begins. (This latter event is experienced in the same manner in this life, which, just like the dream, is a perception.)

This person perceives very sharply the images, sounds, feelings of solidity, light, colours, and all other feelings pertaining to the event he experiences in his dream. The perceptions of his dream are as natural as the ones in "real" life. The cake he eats in his dream satiates him, although it is a mere dream-sense perception, because being satiated is also a dream-sense perception. However, in reality, this person is lying in his bed at that moment. There are no stairs, traffic, or buses to consider. The dreaming person experiences and sees perceptions and feelings that do not exist in the external world. The fact that in our dreams, we experience, see, and feel events with no physical correlates in the "external world" very clearly reveals that the "external world" of our waking lives also consists entirely of mere perceptions. Be it in a dream, or in daily life, all things that are seen, experienced and felt are perceptions.

Let us consider the bus crash example: If the crushed person's nerves travelling from his five senses to his brain, were connected to another person's brain with a parallel connection, at the moment the bus hit him, it would also hit that person sitting at home at the same time. All the feelings experienced by the victim of the accident would be experienced by the person sitting at home, just like the same song being listened to from two different loudspeakers connected to the same tape recorder. That person would feel, see, and experience the braking of the bus, the impact of the bus on his body, the images of a broken arm and blood, fractures, images of his entering the operation room, the hardness of the plaster cast, and the feebleness of his arm.

All other persons connected in parallel to the man's nerves would experience the accident from beginning to end. If the man in the accident fell into a coma, they would all fall into a coma. Moreover, if all the perceptions pertaining to the car accident were recorded, and if all these perceptions were transmitted to someone repeatedly, the bus would knock him down many times.

In dream
you are
having
spiritual
percept-
ion
not
sensory
percept-
ion

For you, reality is all that can be touched with the hand and seen with the eye. In your dreams you can also "touch with your hand and see with your eye", but in reality, then you have neither hand nor eye, nor is there anything that can be touched or seen. There is no material reality that makes these things happen except your brain. You are simply being deceived.
What is it that separates real life and dreams from one another? Ultimately, both forms of living are brought into being within the brain. If we are able to live easily in an unreal world during our dreams, the same can equally be true for the world we live in while awake. When we wake up from a dream, there is no logical reason not to think that we have entered a longer dream called "real life". The reason we consider our dream a fancy and the world 'real' is only a product of our habits and prejudices. This suggests that we may well be awoken from the life on earth, which we think we are living right now, just as we are awoken from a dream.

stupid

So, which one of the buses hitting those people is real? The material-ist philosophy has no consistent answer to this question. The right answer is that they all experience the car accident in all its details in their own minds.

The same principle applies to the cake and stone examples. If the nerves of the sense organs of the person who felt satiety and fullness of his stomach after eating a cake, were connected in parallel, to a second person's brain, the latter would also feel full when the former ate the cake and was satiated. If the nerves of the materialist, who felt pain in his foot when he delivered a sound kick to a stone, were connected in parallel to a second person, the latter would feel the same pain.

So, which cake or which stone is the real one? The materialist philosophy again falls short of giving a consistent answer to this question. The correct and consistent answer is this: both persons have eaten the cake in their minds and are satiated; both persons have fully experienced the moment of striking the stone in their minds.

In that case, it is not possible for man to transcend his senses and break free of them. As in the above-mentioned examples, it is possible to make a man's soul be exposed to all kinds of representations of physical events although they have no physical body and no material existence and lack material weight. It is not possible for a human being to realize this, for he assumes these three-dimensional images to be real and is certain of their existence because, like everybody else, he depends on his sensory organs. It is also clearly revealed in these examples that there is no clear-cut difference between dreams and real life. Therefore, we can never be sure that the life we live now is not a kind of dream.

How could you be then sure that what you believe is right. May be all imagination and product of your mind?

Why Can't They Understand?

The subject we have explained so far is one of the greatest truths that you will ever be told in your lifetime. Proving that the whole material world is in reality a **"shadow being"**, this subject is the key to comprehending the being of God and His creation, and to understanding that He is the only absolute being.

One who understands this subject realizes that the world is not the sort of place it is thought by most people to be. The world is not an absolute place with a true existence as supposed by those who wander aimlessly about the streets, get into fights in pubs, show off in luxurious cafés, spend their lives in vain talk, brag about their property, are caught up in their miserly and selfish passions or who dedicate their lives to hollow aims. The world is only a collection of perceptions, an illusion. All of the people we have alluded to above, no matter what their posts and ranks are, are only shadow beings who watch these perceptions in their minds; yet, remain unaware of this.

The truths explained here are as definite as a law of physics or a chemistry formula. When necessary, people can solve even the most diffi-cult math problems, and grasp many subjects which seem very hard to understand. Yet when the same people are told that matter is nothing but an image formed in the brain, they are reluctant to accept this. This is a very "extreme" case of mindlessness. Grasping the subject in question is as easy as answering such questions as "What is two times two?" or "How old are you?" Or as easy as someone drinking a glass of water would find it to answer the question: "What are you drinking the water out of?" For these are facts definitely proven by science today.

In the field of medicine, if you ask a specialist how the eye works, he can explain to you the technical subjects we have described here in full detail. He, however, does not admit to what is self-evident in consequence of these technical data; he never concedes that "yes, the image is formed in my brain, so it is impossible for me to have a certain idea of what is happening outside." Or if you ask that person, "Where is the moon?" he will look up and say, "The moon is millions of kilometres above." Yet he can never say: "The moon is actually in my brain." He pleads ignorance of it; because to accept this fact or to pronounce it openly reveals another very important fact for him. Since everything is an illusion formed in the brain and presented to him, then there is a Creator Who makes him watch these images.

This is the reason why one who has spent long years in education, and has become known as having the greatest degree of specialization in his own field, from whom many take counsel on a variety of subjects, and who vaunts his intelligence, cannot understand such an obvious reality. This subject reminds such people of religion, calls to mind the being of God, His endless might dominating everything, and that He is the sole Owner of all things. For this reason, Satan influences people not to think about this subject. As stated in the Qur'an with reference to the people of

Saba, "...Satan has made their actions seem good to them and debarred them from the right path so they are not guided to the worship of God." (Surat an-Naml: 24), Satan keeps people at a distance from this fact.

Those influenced by Satan's suggestions are degraded, being unable to see the plain truth before them. Their situation is like that of one who claims that the images on the movie screen "really exist," and who even attempts to intervene in the doings of these images. It is no different from someone stretching out his hand to a plate of food on the TV, taking it to be real. It is evident that the condition of those who try to escape from this subject is a "very extreme state of heedlessness." Indeed, this heedlessness stems from their having been, as disbelievers, bereft of wisdom by God. In the Qur'an, it is stated that disbelievers **"have hearts they do not understand with. They have eyes they do not see with. They have ears they do not hear with. Such people are like cattle. No, they are even further astray! They are the unaware."** (Surat al-A'raf: 179)

The message in the verse is a miracle of the Qur'an. In the Qur'an, God refers to the existence of people who are highly knowledgeable, who can grasp technical subjects, yet who cannot grasp the apparent truth about the real nature of matter despite its having been described to them in various ways. Another verse on this subject predicts their fate:

> As for those who disbelieve, it makes no difference to them whether you warn them or do not warn them, they will not believe. God has sealed up their hearts and hearing and over their eyes is a blindfold. They will have a terrible punishment. (Surat al-Baqarah: 6-7)

Now, God allows some people to grasp this subject. Yet, those who run away from the truth today must know that this scientific fact will, in a few years' time, gain general acceptance in all parts of the world. People will certainly come to understand that they live in an imaginary world put on for them like a play. At a time God has determined, He will remove the veil from the eyes of people and show them that He is the nearest Being to them, that everything save His Being is a "dream." People will fully comprehend this fact about the secret beyond matter, as well as other facts communicated in the Qur'an.

Conclusion

The subject we have explained so far is one of the greatest truths that you will ever be told in your lifetime.

You can explore beyond this point by dint of personal reflection. For this, you have to concentrate upon, devote your attention to, and ponder on the way you see the objects around you and the way you feel their touch. If you think heedfully, you can feel that the intelligent being that sees, hears, touches, thinks, and reads this book at this moment is only a soul, who watches the perceptions called "matter" on a screen. One who comprehends this is considered to have moved away from the domain of the material world that deceives a major part of humanity, and to have entered the domain of true existence.

This reality has been understood by a number of theists and philosophers throughout history. Islamic intellectuals such as Imam Rabbani, Muhyiddin Ibn al-'Arabi and Mawlana Jami realized this from the signs of the Qur'an and by using their reason. Some Western philosophers like George Berkeley have grasped the same reality through reason. Imam Rabbani wrote in his *Maktubat* (Letters) that the whole material universe is an "illusion and supposition (perception)" and that the only absolute being is God:

> God... The substance of these beings which He created is mere nothingness... He created all **in the sphere of senses and illusions...** The existence of the universe is in the sphere of senses and illusions, and it is not material... In reality, there is nothing on the outside except the Glorious Being, (Who is God).[21]

Imam Rabbani explicitly stated that all images presented to man are only illusions, and that they have no originals on the "outside".

> This imaginary cycle is portrayed in imagination. It is seen to the extent that it is portrayed, yet, **with the mind's eye.** On the outside, it seems as if it is seen with the head's eye. However, this is not the case. It has neither a designation nor a trace on the outside. There is no circumstance to be seen. Even the face of a person reflected in a mirror is like that. It has no constancy on the outside. No doubt, both its constancy and image are in the **IMAGINA-**

TION. God knows best.[22]

Mawlana Jami stated the same fact, which he discovered by following the signs of the Qur'an and by using his wit: **"All phenomena of the universe are senses and illusions.** They are either like reflections in mirrors or shadows."

However, the number of those who have understood this fact throughout history has always been limited. Great scholars such as Imam Rabbani have written that it might not be wise to tell this fact to the masses, because most people are not able to grasp it.

In the age in which we live, this has been established as an empirical fact by the body of evidence put forward by science. The fact that the universe is a shadow being is described for the first time in history in such a concrete, clear, and explicit way.

For this reason, **the 21st century** will be **a historical turning point,** when people will generally comprehend the divine realities and be led in crowds to God, the only Absolute Being. The materialistic creeds of the 19th century will be relegated to the trash-heaps of history, God's being and creating will be accepted, spacelessness and timelessness will be understood; humanity, in short, will cast aside the centuries-old veils, deceits and superstitions which have been confusing them.

It is not possible for this unavoidable course to be impeded by any shadow being.

*E*verything related so far demonstrates that "three-dimensional space" does not exist in reality, that it is a prejudice completely founded on perceptions and that one leads one's whole life in "spacelessness." For there is no valid proof of the existence of a three-dimensional, material world. The universe we inhabit is a sum of images made up of plays of light and shade. To assert the contrary would be to hold a superstitious belief far removed from reason and scientific truth.

This refutes the primary assumption of the materialist philosophy, the assumption that matter is absolute and eternal. The second assumption, upon which materialistic philosophy rests, is the supposition that time is absolute and eternal. This is as superstitious as the first.

The Perception of Time

What we perceive as time is, in fact, a method by which one moment is compared to another. We can explain this with an example. For instance, when a person taps an object, he hears a particular sound. When he taps the same object five minutes later, he hears another sound. He perceives that there is an interval between the first sound and the second, and he calls this interval "time." Yet at the time he hears the second sound, the first sound he heard is no more than a mental imagining. It is merely a bit of information in his memory. The person formulates the concept of "time" by **comparing the moment in which he lives with what he has in his memory. If this comparison is not made, there can be no concept of time.**

Similarly, the occupant of a room makes a comparison when he sees someone enter through a door and sit in an armchair in the middle of the room. By the time the newcomer sits in the armchair, the images related to the moments he opens the door, walks into the room, and makes his way to the armchair are compiled as bits of information in his brain. The perception of time occurs when he compares the man sitting in the armchair with those bits of information.

In brief, **time comes to exist as a result of the comparison made between some illusions stored in the brain.** If man did not have memory, his brain would not make such interpretations and he would never therefore have formed the concept of time. The only reason why someone determines himself to be thirty years old is because he has accumulated information pertaining to those thirty years in his mind. If his memory did not exist, then he would not think of the existence of such a preceding period, and he would only experience the single "moment" in which he lives — which is a very important point.

The Scientific Explanation of Timelessness

Let us try to clarify the subject by quoting various scientists' and scholars' explanations of the subject. Regarding the subject of time flowing backwards, the famous intellectual and Nobel laureate professor of genetics, François Jacob, states the following in his book *Le Jeu des Possibles* (The Possible and the Actual):

> Films played backwards make it possible for us to imagine **a world in which time flows backwards**. A world in which milk separates itself from the coffee and jumps out of the cup to reach the milk-pan; a world in which light rays are emitted from the walls to be collected in a trap (gravity center) instead of gushing out from a light source; a world in which a stone slopes to the palm of a man by the astonishing cooperation of innumerable drops of water which enable the stone to jump out of water. Yet, in such a world in which time has such opposite features, **the processes of our brain and the way our memory compiles information, would similarly be functioning backwards.** The same is true for the past and future and the world will appear to us exactly as it currently appears.[23]

Since our brain is accustomed to a certain sequence of events, the world does not operate as is related above and we assume that time has always flowed forward. However, this is a decision reached in the brain and is relative. Had the bits of information in our memory been arranged as in films played backwards, for us, the flow of time would be as in these films played backwards. In this situation, we would start to perceive the past as the future, and the future as the past, and live our lives in a totally opposite sequence.

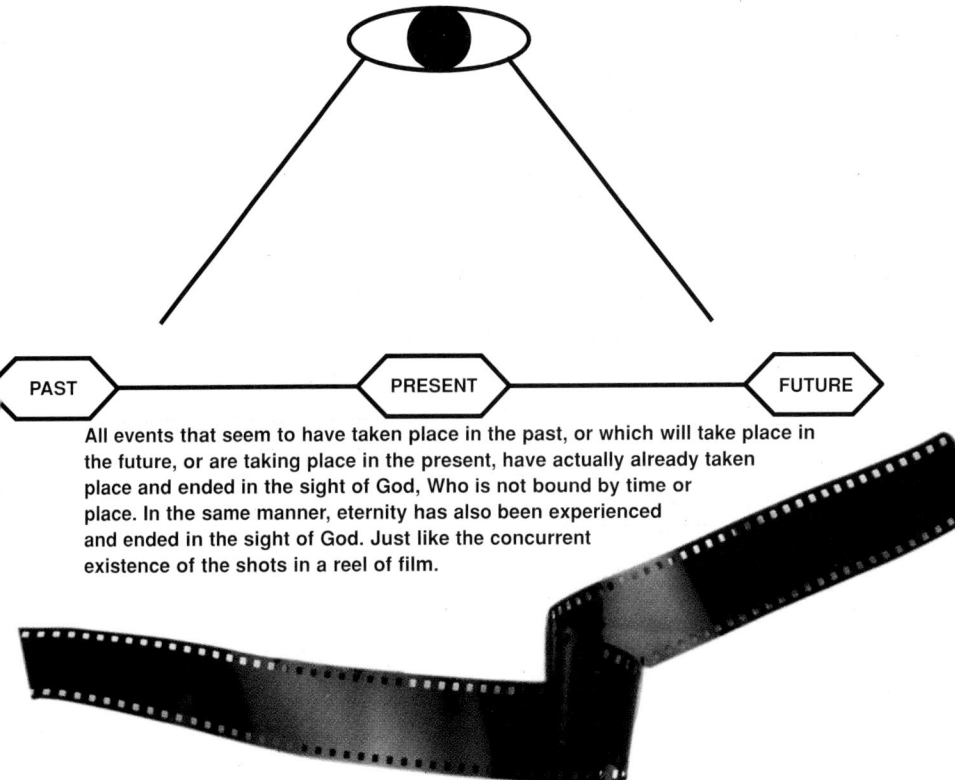

PAST — **PRESENT** — **FUTURE**

All events that seem to have taken place in the past, or which will take place in the future, or are taking place in the present, have actually already taken place and ended in the sight of God, Who is not bound by time or place. In the same manner, eternity has also been experienced and ended in the sight of God. Just like the concurrent existence of the shots in a reel of film.

In reality, we can never know how time flows or even whether it flows or not. This is an indication of **the fact that time is not an absolute fact, but just a sort of perception.**

The relativity of time is a fact also verified by one of the most important physicists of the 20th century, Albert Einstein. Lincoln Barnett writes in his book *The Universe and Dr. Einstein*:

Along with absolute space, Einstein discarded the concept of absolute time – of a steady, unvarying inexorable universal time flow, streaming from the infinite past to the infinite future. Much of the obscurity that has surrounded the Theory of Relativity stems from man's reluctance to recognize that **sense of time, like sense of colour, is a form of perception**. Just as space is simply a possible order of material objects, so **time is simply a possible order of events.** The subjectivity of time is best explained in Einstein's own words. "The experiences of an individual" he says, "appear to us arranged in a series of events; **in this series the single events which we remember appear to be ordered according to the criterion of 'earlier' and 'later'.** There exists, therefore, for the individual, an I-time, or **subjective time.** This in itself is not measurable. I can, indeed, associate numbers with the events, in such a way that a greater number is associated with the later event than with an earlier one."[24]

Einstein himself pointed out, as quoted in Barnett's book: "Space and time are forms of intuition, **which can no more be divorced from consciousness** than can our concepts of colour, shape, or size." According to the Theory of General Relativity: **"Time has no independent existence apart from the order of events by which we measure it."**[25]

Since time is based on perception, it depends entirely on the perceiver and is therefore relative.

The speed at which time flows differs according to the references we use to measure it, because there is no natural clock in the human body to indicate precisely how fast time passes. As Lincoln Barnett wrote: "Just as there is no such thing as colour without an eye to discern it, so an instant or an hour or a day is nothing without an event to mark it."[26]

The relativity of time is plainly experienced in dreams. Although what we see in our dreams seems to last for hours, in fact, it only lasts for a few minutes, and even a few seconds.

Let us think about an example to clarify the subject further. Let us assume that we were put in a room with a single specially designed window and we were kept there for a certain period. A clock in the room would allow us to see the amount of time that had passed. At the same time, we are able to see from the window of the room the sun rising and setting at certain intervals. A few days later, the answer we would give to the question about the length of time we had spent in the room would be based both on the information we had collected by looking at the clock from time to time and on the computation we had made by referring to how many times the sun had risen and set. Suppose, we estimate that we spent three days in the room. However, if the person who put us in that room said that we spent only two days there and that the sun we had seen from the window was produced artificially by a simulation machine and that the clock in the room was regulated specially to work faster, then the calculation we had done would have no meaning.

This example confirms that the information we have about the rate of the passage of time is based on relative references.

In the same manner, the fact that everyone perceives the flowing speed of time differently under different situations is evidence that time is but a psychological perception. For instance, when you have to meet a friend, a 10-minute delay on his part would seem to you like an interminable, or at least a very long time. Or for a sleepless person who has to wake up to go to school or work, an

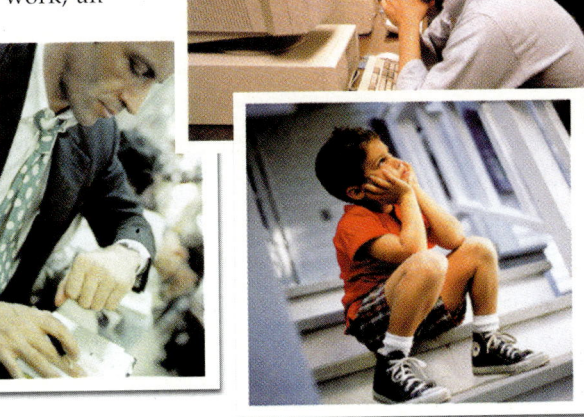

Time is a psychological perception. It can be perceived differently by different people in different circumstances.

extra ten-minute sleep may seem very long. He may even think that he has had all his sleep in these ten minutes. In some circumstances, just the opposite happens. As you would remember from your school years, after a forty-minute lesson which seems to last for centuries, a ten minutes break may seem to pass very quickly.

The relativity of time is a scientific fact also proven by scientific methodology. **Einstein's Theory of General Relativity** maintains that the speed of time changes depending on the speed of the object and its position in the gravitational field. As speed increases, time is shortened and compressed: it slows down as if coming to the point of "stopping."

Let us explain this with an example given by Einstein. Imagine twins, one of whom stays on earth while the other goes travelling in space at a speed close to that of light. When he comes back, the traveller will see that his brother has grown much older than he has. The reason is that time flows much more slowly for the person who travels at speeds near the speed of light. The same applies to a father travelling in space in a rocket, the speed of which is close to ninety-nine per cent of the speed of light, and his earth-bound son. If the father were twenty-seven years old when he set out and his son three; when the father came back to earth thirty years later (earth time), the son would be thirty-three years old while his father would be only thirty.[27] *1 year of father = 10 years of son*

This relativity of time is not caused by the deceleration or acceleration of clocks, or the deceleration of a mechanical spring. It is rather the result of the differentiated operation periods of the entire system of material existence, which goes as deep as sub-atomic particles. In other words, for the person experiencing it, the shortening of time is not experienced as if acting in a slow-motion picture. In such a setting where time shortens, one's heartbeats, cell replica-

> *Truly, a day in the sight of your Lord is like a thousand years of your reckoning.*
> *(Surat al-Hajj: 47)*

tions, and brain functions, etc, all operate more slowly. Nevertheless, the person goes on with his daily life and does not notice the shortening of time at all.

These facts revealed by the Theory of Relativity have been verified quite a few times by various scientists. In his book *Frontiers*, Isaac Asimov also states that it is 84 years since the publication of Einstein's Theory of Relativity, and each time the theory has been tested, Einstein has been proved right once again.[28]

Relativity in the Qur'an

The conclusion to which we are led by the findings of modern science is that **time is not an absolute fact as supposed by materialists, but only a relative perception.** What is most interesting is that this fact, undiscovered until the 20th century by science, was revealed to mankind in the Qur'an fourteen centuries ago. There are various references in the Qur'an to the relativity of time.

It is possible to see in many verses of the Qur'an the scientifically proven fact that time is a psychological perception dependent on events, setting, and conditions. For instance, a person's entire life is a very short time, as we are informed in the Qur'an:

> On the Day when He will call you, you will answer His Call with words of His Praise and Obedience, and you will think that you have stayed in this world but a little while! (Surat al-Isra': 52)

> And on the Day when He shall gather them together, it will seem to them as if they had not tarried on earth longer than an hour of a day: they will recognize each other. (Surah Yunus: 45)

Some verses indicate that people perceive time differently and that sometimes people can perceive a very short period as a very lengthy one. The following conversation of people held during their judgment in the hereafter is a good example of this:

> He will say: "What number of years did you stay on earth?" They will say: "We stayed a day or part of a day, but ask those who keep account." He

will say: "Brief indeed was your sojourn, if you had only known!" (Surat al-Mu'minun: 112-114)

In some other verses God states that time may flow at different paces in different settings:

...Truly, a day in the sight of your Lord is like a thousand years of your reckoning. (Surat al-Hajj: 47)

The angels and the spirit ascend to Him in a day the measure of which is like fifty thousand years. (Surat al-Ma'arij: 4) *(by your reckoning)*

He rules all affairs from the heavens to the earth: in the end all will ascend to Him in a single day, the measure of which is a thousand years by your reckoning. (Surat as-Sajdah: 5)

These verses are clear expressions of the relativity of time. That this finding, which was only recently understood by scientists in the 20th century, was communicated to man 1,400 years ago in the Qur'an is an indication of the revelation of the Qur'an by God, Who encompasses the whole of time and space.

Many other verses of the Qur'an reveal that time is a perception. This is particularly evident in the stories. For instance, God kept the Companions of the Cave, a group of believers mentioned in the Qur'an, in a deep sleep for more than three centuries. When they awoke, these people thought that they had stayed in that state for only a little while, and could not reckon how long they had slept:

Then We drew (a veil) over their ears, for a number of years, in the Cave, (so that they could not hear). Then We wakened them up so that We might know which of the two parties would best calculate the time that they had tarried. (Surat al-Kahf: 11-12)

Such being their state, We roused them from sleep, so that they might question each other. Said one of them, "How long have you stayed (here)?" They said, "We have stayed perhaps a day, or part of a day." At length they all said, "God alone knows best how long you have stayed here..." (Surat al-Kahf: 19)

The situation described in the verse below is also evidence that time is in truth a psychological perception.

> Or (take) the instance of one who passed by a hamlet, all desolate and in ruins. He said, "How shall God ever bring it to life now that is dead?" but God caused him to die for a hundred years, then brought him back to life. He said: "How long did you tarry thus?" He said: Perhaps a day or part of a day." He said: "No, you have tarried thus a hundred years; but look at your food and your drink; they show no signs of age; and look at your donkey. And so that We may make of you a sign to the people, look further at the bones, how We bring them together and clothe them with flesh." When this was shown clearly to him, he said: "I know that God has power over all things." (Surat al-Baqarah: 259)

The above verse clearly emphasizes that God, Who created time, is unbound by it. Man, on the other hand, is bound by time, which is ordained by God. As in the verse, man is even incapable of knowing how long he has slept. This being so, to assert that time is absolute (just as materialists do in their distorted thinking) is very unreasonable.

Destiny

This relativity of time clears up a very important matter. Relativity is so variable that a period appearing to us to be billions of years' in duration may last only a second in another perspective. Moreover, an enormous period of time, extending from the world's beginning to its end, may not even last a second but just an instant in another dimension.

This is the very essence of the concept of destiny – a concept that is not well understood by most people, especially materialists who deny it completely. Destiny is God's perfect knowledge of all events past or future. A majority of people question how God can already know events that have not yet been experienced and this leads them to fail to understand the authenticity of destiny. However, "events not yet experienced" are only so **for us**. God is not bound by time or space, for He Himself has created them. For this reason, **past, future, and present are all the same to God; for Him everything has already taken place and finished**.

In *The Universe and Dr. Einstein*, Lincoln Barnett explains how the

Theory of General Relativity leads to this conclusion. According to Barnett, the universe can be **"encompassed in its entire majesty only by a cosmic intellect."** The will that Barnett calls "the cosmic intellect" is **the wisdom and knowledge of God, Who prevails over the entire universe.** Just as we can easily see a ruler's beginning, middle, and end, and all the units in between as a whole, God knows the time we are subject to as if it were a single moment right from its beginning to its end. People, however, experience incidents only when their time comes and they witness the destiny God has created for them.

It is also important to draw attention to the shallowness of the distorted understanding of destiny prevalent in our society. This distorted belief about fate is a superstition that God has determined a "destiny" for every man, but that people can sometimes change these destinies. For instance, people make superficial statements about a patient who returns from death's door, such as "he defeated his destiny." No one is able to change his destiny. The person, who returned from death's door, didn't die precisely because he was destined not to die at that time. It is, ironically, the destiny of those people who deceive themselves by saying "I defeated my destiny" that they should say so and maintain such a mindset. In the verse, **"…no living thing lives long or has its life cut short without that being in a Book. That is easy for God"** (Surah Fatir: 11), it is stated that all things happen as a matter of destiny. Destiny is the eternal knowledge of God and for God, Who knows time like a single moment and Who prevails over the whole of time and space; everything is determined and finished in destiny.

We also understand from what He relates in the Qur'an that time is one for God: some incidents that appear to us to happen in the future are related in the Qur'an as if they had already taken place long before. For instance, the verses that describe the accounts that people must give to God in the hereafter are related as events which occurred long ago:

> **And the trumpet is blown, and all who are in the heavens and all who are on the earth swoon away, save him whom God wills. Then it is blown a second time, and behold them standing waiting! And the earth shone**

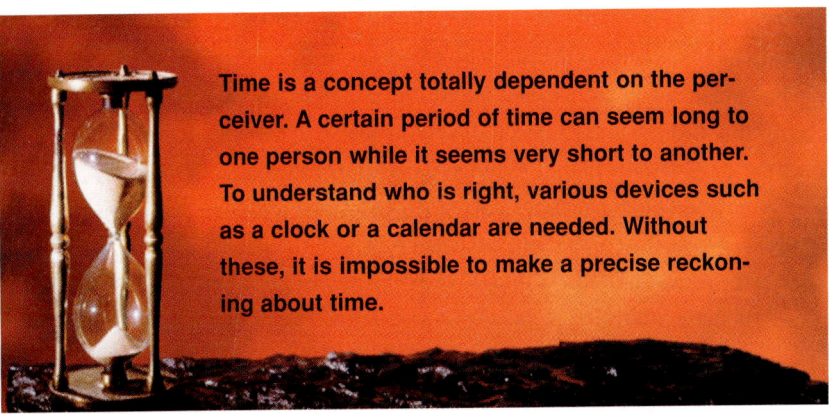

Time is a concept totally dependent on the perceiver. A certain period of time can seem long to one person while it seems very short to another. To understand who is right, various devices such as a clock or a calendar are needed. Without these, it is impossible to make a precise reckoning about time.

with the light of her Lord, and the Book is set up, and the prophets and the witnesses are brought, and it is judged between them with truth, and they are not wronged... And those who disbelieve are driven into hell in troops... And those who feared their Lord are driven into Paradise in troops... (Surat az-Zumar: 68-73)

Some other verses on this subject are:

And every soul came, along with a driver and a witness. (Surat al-Qaf: 21)

And the heaven is cloven asunder, so that on that day it is frail. (Surat al-Haqqah: 16)

And because they were patient and constant, He rewarded them with a garden and garments of silk. Reclining in the garden on raised thrones, they saw there neither the sun's excessive heat nor excessive cold. (Surat al-Insan: 12-13)

And Hell is placed in full view for all to see. (Surat an-Nazi'at: 36)

But on this day the believers laugh at the unbelievers (Surat al-Mutaffifin: 34)

And the sinful saw the fire and realised they are going to fall into it and find no way of escaping from it. (Surat al-Kahf: 53)

As may be seen, occurrences that are going to take place after our death (from our point of view) are related in the Qur'an as past events already experienced. God is not bound by the relative time frame in which we are confined. God has willed these things in timelessness: people have already performed them and all these events have been lived through and are ended. He states in the verse below that every event, big or small, is within the knowledge of God and recorded in a book:

> In whatever business you may be, and whatever portion you may be reciting from the Qur'an, and whatever deed you (mankind) may be doing, We are witnesses of these things when you are deeply engrossed in them. Nor is there hidden from your Lord so much as the weight of an atom on the earth or in heaven. And there is neither the least and nor the greatest of these things but is recorded in a glorious book. (Surah Yunus: 61)

The Gain of Believers

The issues discussed in this chapter, namely the truth underlying matter, timelessness, and spacelessness, are indeed extremely clear. As expressed before, these are definitely not any sort of philosophy or way of thought, but **scientific outcomes that are impossible to deny.** In addition to its being a technical reality, the evidence also admits of no other rational or logical alternatives on this issue: **the universe is an illusory entity** with all the matter composing it and all the creatures living in it. It is a collection of perceptions.

Materialists have a hard time understanding this issue. The basic reason why materialists cannot comprehend this subject is their subliminal fear of what they will face when they comprehend it. Lincoln Barnett tells us that some scientists "discerned" this point:

> Along with philosophers' reduction of all objective reality to a shadow-world of perceptions, scientists have become aware of the **alarming limita-**

As for those who do not believe in God's Signs, God will not guide them and they will have a painful punishment. (Surat an-Nahl: 104)

tions of man's senses.[29]

While the fact that matter and time are perceptions alarms materialists, the opposite holds true for believers. People of faith become very
glad when they perceive the secret beyond matter, because this reality is
the key to all questions. With this key, all secrets are unlocked. One comes
easily to understand many issues that one previously had difficulty in
addressing.

As said before, the questions of death, paradise, hell, the hereafter,
changing dimensions, and questions such as "Where is God?" "What was
before God?" "Who created God?" "How long will life in the grave last?"
"Where are heaven and hell?" and "Where do heaven and hell currently
exist?" are easily answered. It will be understood with what kind of order
God created the entire universe from out of nothing, so much so that, with
this secret, **the questions of "when?" and "where?" become meaningless**
because there are no time or space left. When spacelessness is grasped, it
will be understood that **hell, heaven, and earth are all actually the same
place**. When timelessness is grasped, it will be understood that everything takes place **at a single moment**: nothing is waited for and time does
not go by, because everything has already happened and finished. **That
means that in truth, eternity has already begun.** *Eternity does not have a beginning*

With this secret out in the open, **the world becomes like heaven for
a believer.** All distressful material worries, anxieties, and fears vanish. He
grasps that the entire universe has a single sovereign, that He changes the
entire physical world as He pleases and that all one has to do is to turn to
Him. He then submits himself entirely to God **"to be devoted to His service."** (Surat Al 'Imran: 35)

To comprehend this secret is the greatest gain in the world.

Eternity Has Already Begun

The Limited Memory of Man and the Endless Memory of God

*I*n the section related to timelessness, we mentioned that all our information is in the memory. All the details pertaining to one's life, everything one sees, hears, knows or feels are bits of memorized information. So are our sensations about time. Now, we will deal with the concept of memory more fully.

As mentioned in the preceding pages, we rely on our five senses to live. We perceive only what our senses allow and we can never succeed in stepping out of the boundaries of our senses. The time and space we live in is similarly perceived. If our brain cannot detect a being through our five senses, we simply say that that being has "disappeared." Accordingly, for us, events, images or sensations, which are stored in our memory, exist, i.e., they are alive, while those that are forgotten no longer exist. To put it another way, beings and events, which are not in our memory, become past events for us; they are simply dead and non-existent.

Yet, this holds true only for human beings; that is because it is only human beings who have a limited memory. The memory of God, on the other hand, is superior to everything. It is boundless and eternal. Yet one point deserves mention here: the concept "the memory of God" is used only for clarification purposes. It is definitely unlikely that any comparison or similarity could be drawn between the memory of God and the memory of a man. God is surely the One Who creates everything from nothingness and Who knows everything down to the last detail.

God introduces Himself in His book through His attributes. One of them is al- Hafiz (The Preserver), "He Who preserves all things in detail" Behind this attribute, there are very important hidden mysteries.

"The Mother of the Book"

In the sight of God, everything has taken place and finished in a moment. Since the beginning of time, everything has taken place at this single moment. In the sight of God, all information pertaining to this moment is kept in a "Book." This "Main Book", or as the Qur'an calls it, "The Mother of the Book", holds every bit of information about everything:

And truly, it is in the Mother of the Book, in Our Presence, high in dignity, and full of wisdom. (Surat az-Zukhruf: 4)

... with Him is the Mother of the Book. (Surat ar-Ra'd: 39)

We possess an all-preserving Book (Surah Qaf: 4)

Certainly there is no hidden thing in either heaven or earth which is not in a Clear Book. (Surat An-Naml: 75)

And the Book (of Deeds) will be placed (before you); and you will see the sinful in great terror because of what is recorded therein; they will say, "Alas for us! What a Book is this! It leaves out nothing small or great, but takes account thereof!" They will find all that they did, placed before them and your Lord will not wrong anyone at all. (Surat al-Kahf: 49)

In other verses, too, God declares that all the events one experiences, all the thoughts one considers, and everything that befalls one are included in this Book:

No misfortune can happen on earth or in your souls without its being in a Book before We bring it into existence: That is truly easy for God. (Surat al-Hadid: 22)

Actually everything, living or non-living, which has existed since the beginning of the universe and all events, which have happened, have all been created by God. Consequently, God is cognizant of them all. To put it in another way, "They all exist in the memory of God." In this sense, the Mother of the Book is a manifestation of God's attribute, the al-Hafiz.

At this point, we come upon a striking fact: because the memory of God is infinite, nothing existent in Him becomes lost. In other words, no living being created by God vanishes, no flower fades, no drink finishes, no period comes to an end, and no food is consumed. Every moment God creates and every exact detail of everything are created in eternity and it is "destined to eternity."

What then does this phrase "destined to eternity" mean?

Every moment pertaining to the collapse of these buildings is kept in the sight of God.

Let us put this explanation in the following way: eternity has begun for a being or an event by the time it is created. For instance, when a flower is created, it is, in reality, destined not to disappear. That this being ceases to become a part of one's sensations and is erased from one's memory does not actually mean that it has vanished or died. Its state in the sight of God is what actually matters. Furthermore, all states of this being, be it its creation, all moments throughout its life or death, do exist in the memory of God.

Upon all that is created, God bestows eternity. In other words, existing things have attained eternity by the time they are created. To have a thorough grasp of this notion, however, one needs to reflect on all beings and events individually. But, before proceeding with this subject, it would be useful to stress the following fact: what has been stated so far, together with the following, is no doubt the most important information one can ever acquire in one's lifetime. Most probably, many people are hearing and reflecting on these facts about timelessness for the first time in their lives. However, here is something important to keep in mind: God, in the Qur'an, draws our attention to the fact that **"only those who sincerely turn to God"** take heed. In other words, only those who truly seek the guidance of God and endeavour to appreciate His infinite might and His greatness will heed these explanations and have a grasp of these facts.

People in Eternity

God, the al-Khalig (the Creator), is the One Who creates everything from nothing and Who creates all things with the knowledge of what will happen to them. As a manifestation of this attribute of God, by the time He creates man in his mother's womb, eternity has begun for him. Surely, man does not recall the stages of his own development in the womb. However, every moment of this progress is present in the sight of God and they quite definitely never disappear. Similarly, it is unlikely that those initial phases and developmental stages of a human being remain in his memory. Unless informed by God, man never manages to see these moments. Some moments, however, remain only as memories. The moments we experience are purely sensations presented to our soul. Yet, in the infinite memory of God, everything remains as it is. Everything people encounter in life, all details pertaining to one's experiences, are all created by God and they never disappear. As stated in the following verse, everything down to its last detail remains in the sight of God.

> ".... This is so you will know that God knows what is in the heavens and in the earth and God has knowledge of all things." (Surat al-Ma'idah: 97)

Let's take the Prophet Adam as an example; all the details pertaining to Adam's creation in paradise before he was sent to earth, and the way he was tested in paradise are all present in the Main Book. Adam's initial creation from clay, the angels' prostration to him, as well as the moment he was sent to earth and all the events he experienced are all vivid and existing right now. None of them has disappeared, they all exist right now in the sight of God, right down to their finest details.

As another example, let's think of someone who is sorry for the death of his cat. In fact, the moment the cat died and the period that that same cat was still a kitten, in fact, its entire development from the moment of its birth are kept vivid in the memory of God. Besides, the moments the owner of this cat when he was at work or all the moments he did not spend with the cat are vividly stored in the sight of God. Consequently, death does not put an end to the existence of a being. For all eternity, everything exists in the sight of God.

Likewise, the moment the Prophet Solomon (Sulayman) caressed the legs of his horse remains forever. The disappearance of these horses behind a curtain, the letter the Prophet Solomon sent to the Queen of Saba, the moment this letter is read by the Queen and her soldiers, how the Queen is welcomed to the palace of Solomon, the moment she thought the ground of the palace to be a lake and the words of the Queen: **"I do now submit in Islam, with Solomon, to the Lord of the Worlds."** (Surat an-Naml: 44) currently exist and will continue to exist for all eternity.

These examples deserve a deeper and more detailed reflection. Assume that in the time of the Prophet Noah (Nuh), a man's shirt became unravelled and that after sometime a tailor sewed it up. This shirt, the loom on which it was initially woven, the state of the shirt before it became unravelled and the state in which it was sewed, and even every second the tailor spent on using the needle to sew this shirt, the process by which this shirt became utterly unusable, in brief, every stage, every second, every moment the shirt went through are retained in the sight of God. Right at this moment, this shirt is being woven, it is still sewn and it is still worn by its owner who lived in the time of the Prophet Noah.

Let's also think about the antique clock in your home. All the stages of manufacturing which took place 200 years ago along with the manufacturing stages of a single wire in the clock, the moment its hour and minute hand were placed in it, the time this clock was sold to a shop and a customer purchased it, then the moment the clock went out of order and was given to a rag-and-bone man, the moment your grand-grandfather purchased it from him and the time this clock was inherited first by your grand father and then your father, and then you, the way you placed the clock in your living room and watched it with admiration, briefly, every second in the history of the clock still remain in the sight of God. In absolute terms, this clock is working right at this moment, it has stopped again right now, it is being placed by you in your living room and it is purchased by your grandfather at this moment. All these happenings are present in the memory of God. Furthermore, not only what the clock went through in the past but also its every future-related moment — surely this is the "future" for you — is known by God and is preserved in His sight. The way this clock will be placed in your son's home in forty years' time and the collapse of the clock in three hundred years' time is also included in the Mother of the Book.

The verse "**He knows what is in front of them and what is behind them. But their knowledge does not encompass Him." (Surah Ta ha: 110)** refers to this fact (Surely God knows best). That is because God knows every being moment by moment. He knows their previous states as well as their latter states, that is, in the words of the Qur'an, "what is in front of them and what is behind them", at all stages. In another verse, God once again reminds us of the fact that everything is within His Knowledge;

God - Him from Whom nothing is hidden, either on earth or in heaven. (Surat Al 'Imran: 5)

For someone who crosses the street from one side to the other, there is a certain distance to be crossed. A person, however, who looks at this street from a bird's eye view, feels no difficulty in seeing every point in this street from one end to another.

All Events Are Happening Right At This Moment!

An example will lead us to a better understanding of the fact that, in the sight of God, every incident takes place in a single moment. Assume that you have the picture of a big city spread in front of you. Streets, vehicles, buildings lined up side by side and people are clearly seen in this picture. Let's also imagine that there is a man trying to reach the other end of this city. From the point of view of this man, there is a certain distance to be crossed from one end of this city to another in a definite time. It surely takes some time for this man to reach his destination. It is unlikely that he can be present at two distinct places at the same time. Yet, this is not the case for a person like you who looks at this picture from the outside. At a first glance, you can see all the details of the city in a single moment. Moreover, you do not even need a specific time in which to do this.

This state outlined in the above example also holds true for people

like us confined to a specific dimension. For us, reaching a destination becomes possible only with the passage of time and by expending some energy. However, for God, the Creator of all dimensions, it takes only a single moment for all events to occur.

The second important fact is **the simultaneity** of these events. As stated earlier, in the sight of God, it is not possible to

is seen to

talk about the notion of time; everything takes place and ends in a single instant.

The Prophet Adam is created from clay right **at this moment**, angels are prostrating themselves before the Prophet Adam right **now**. Likewise, he is **now** being sent to earth. Furthermore, the "moment" we are talking about is the "moment" you are reading these lines.

Another example will further clarify this explanation. Let's think about the Prophet Moses (Musa). The moment his mother decided to place the baby Moses in a box and set him adrift on the water is still present; that moment never disappeared and will continue to exist forever. The moment the Prophet Moses went to Pharaoh (Fir'awn) and conveyed the message of God to him still exists. In reality, just at this moment, the Prophet Moses is inviting Pharaoh to accept the religion of truth. It is a fact that this is also **the moment** the Prophet Moses is receiving the revelations of God in the sacred valley of Tuwa. It is also **this instant** the Prophet Moses is running away from Pharaoh with his people, and at this moment the Red sea opens a way for the Prophet Moses and his people to walk across. For all eternity, this moment when the sea opens will remain and exist in God's memory.

Moment by moment, every picture above shows an image of the vehicle crossing the bridge. A person travelling by this vehicle supposes that a particular period of time is spent in crossing the bridge. However, we can see all of these pictures at a single moment.

The moment Mary became pregnant, the moment she gave birth to Prophet Jesus ('Isa) under a date palm, the moment she returned to her people, the moment the Prophet Jesus talked to them while he was still in his cradle, as well as the moment he asked the question **"Who will be my helpers to God?"** to his disciples, and was resurrected by God, are all happening right at this moment. Indeed, not only the past events we are familiar with, but also the ones of which we have no idea because they will happen in the future are, in reality, happening just at this moment. Every second the Prophet Jesus spent in this world, his communication of the message of God to his disciples, his return to the earth, every speech he delivered to call people to the path of God, his death and his resurrection on the Day of Judgement as well as the moments he will be greeted by angels in his entrance to Heaven are actually happening at this moment.

Each incident, each moment in timelessness exists simultaneously everywhere and will continue to exist for all eternity. None of the moments, none of the events, none of the living beings which existed in the past have disappeared, nor will they ever disappear. The Prophet Noah is building the ark right at this moment. The flood at the time of Noah, too, is making its impact right now; everything, every moment related to the flood is taking place during the time you read these lines. These are certainly not the incidents of the past. The ongoing events, as well as the aforementioned incidents, all happen at the same time, since each one of them is fated to remain in the memory of God for all eternity.

The same also holds true for someone who lived 3,000 years ago. A man who sat under a tree at noontime in 3000 BC, reflecting on a ladybird perched on his finger and who therefore glorified the creation of God, is actually performing these actions right at this moment. Moreover, the moment the ladybird returned to its nest, as well as all the phases the ladybird went through, from the moment it was in its egg to its death, are all kept in the memory of God. Consequently, all these happen in a single moment, at the very moment you are reading this passage.

All these examples indicate, once again, an important fact: None of the moments, none of the events, none of the living beings which existed in the past ceased to exist and they will never disappear. A film we watch on television is recorded on a filmstrip and the moving pictures composing the film are not lost, whether we watch them or not. The same thing also holds true for each and everything which has to do with life relating to the past or future.

It is essential that this point should be well grasped. None of these occurrences are similar to a memory, reminiscence or an image. They are all vivid, everything being preserved as it is, and are just like the moment we experience right now. We perceive them as incidents of the past simply because God does not present these perceptions to us. However, whenever He wills, God may display these images to us, making us believe that we truly experience them.

Past, Present and Future; they are All the Same

As has already been clarified, in the sight of God, all events, which have occurred on earth so far, take place at a single moment. What the Prophets Moses, Abraham (Ibrahim), Noah, Solomon, and Muhammad, together with all the other prophets, went through is experienced in the time we actually live in. Likewise, the experiences of our grandsons, of their grandsons, as well as of all the people who will live until the Judgement Day take place at one and the same moment. Among these people those who believe are now in heaven, while the disbelievers are in hell, suffering agonies.

What our Prophet went through, too, will remain in the sight of God forever. These events are presented to our sensations as if they happened 1400 years ago. However, the truth is, **right at this moment**, our Prophet Muhammad is ascending to heaven, right now, he is taking refuge in the cave with his friend. Again, **this is the moment** our Prophet is communicating the message of God to disbelievers. Actually these are not events, which occurred in the past. On the contrary, they are incidents doomed to exist for all eternity. The reason why we do not see, witness or experience these events is simply because they are not present in our memory.

The same thing holds true for all the events that took place and the people who appeared on earth throughout history. Philosophers in ancient Greece, those Sumerian people who invented cuneiform writing, Cleopatra, the Egyptian Queen, artists of the renaissance period, scientists of the 19th century, dictators of the 20th century and all other people, even your grandfather, his grandgrandfather and you are, in reality, living at the same moment.

None of these events disappear; they continue to exist without changing. The Crusades, the great migration, World Wars I and II, though seemingly distinct historical events, are actually events happening right at this moment and they will continue to do so for all eternity. Likewise, Egyptian, ancient Mexican, Greek and Anatolian civilisations all existed at the same moment.

The rain, which watered the

All construction stages of these buildings as well as their current state are in the sight of God. Every deed engaged in by the former dwellers of these buildings is kept "right now" in the sight of God.

field of a man who earned his living as a farmer in 1000 BC in Mesopotamia, and the very moment this farmer got wet in this rain are also present in the sight of God. A spider which wove a net in the branches of a willow in the Akkadian period is, likewise, weaving this net just now. The same spider, in a corner of this net, is also waiting for its prey right at this moment. Furthermore, the very same moment you try to visualise this spider in your mind, it is laying its eggs, collecting them on its back, and also taking care of them. Also, at this very moment, the eggs are cracking and its many offspring are hatching.

Nothing is left out or forgotten; the creation of God serves various purposes. So, nothing disappears, vanishes or is wasted. That people do not see, know or experience these various occurrences does not mean that they are not happening right now. As God is unbounded by time, everything has already taken place and finished in His sight. However, being bound by time, the experiences of an individual appear to be arranged in a series of events the order of which is apparently based on the criterion of the past, the present and the future. However, as also mentioned earlier, "events not yet experienced" are not "yet experienced" for us. Past, future and present are all the same to God. That is why God knows everything. This fact is also stated in the following verse:

> "My son!" (said Luqman), "Even if something weighs as little as a mustard-seed and is inside a rock or anywhere else in the heavens or earth, God will bring it out. God is All-Pervading, All-Aware." (Surah Luqman: 16)

Your Life is Also a Single Moment

To comprehend this fact, there is no reason to ponder merely upon events or wander in the realms of history. One's life, which he assumes to be long, too, is nothing but a moment. That first moment you were born, and the moment your mother embraced you for the first time still exist. That single square or that event will continue to exist for all eternity because it is stored in the memory of God. Yet, as stated earlier, because all the information that you have about the world is conveyed to you by your five senses, and because you have such a dependency on your senses and no information pertaining to this image is kept in your memory, you do not see such a scene. This is true of everything you experience in life. The day you enrolled in primary school, one of the birthdays you celebrated, an event you experienced, the day you graduated from high school, your wedding day and similar other "turning points" in your life are each, in the sight of God, merely a moment. None of these events disappeared; they will exist forever.

Similarly, the sweet taste you discovered in chocolate when you were only a five year old, the anxiety you felt when you woke up to the first day of the primary school, the boredom you felt in one of the classes in high school, the difficult equations your maths teacher wrote on the blackboard, the pain you felt when you lost a close a friend in a traffic accident, the pride you took in your academic accomplishments, the glow of happiness you felt when you succeeded in having something you had dreamed of for years, in brief, all your experiences and feelings remain just as they were; they are not simply kept in your memory. You perceive what is kept in

The human being in the picture is being born "right now"; he is fishing, he is receiving his diploma, getting married and even having children and grandchildren "right at this moment." Furthermore, he is dying now and likewise, he is being judged in the sight of God.

your memory simply as memory or the past. Though they exist right now, the brain does not perceive these scenes, since this is the way man is being tested on earth. Believing they are bound by a steady, unvarying time flow, streaming from the past to the future, people assume their lives are divided into distinct sections, namely, past, present and future. This actually poses a major hindrance to their grasp of particular events like the existence of the hereafter, when and where paradise, hell and the day of judgement will take place. They cannot relate the concept of time in the sight of God to the concept of time people are bound by. However, knowing that every living being, every event and everything is created eternally square by square just like the squares making up a film roll and brought into being simultaneously will make it easier to comprehend this issue.

In the sight of God, everything has already taken place and finished. Some people hold the superstitious belief that God created the universe and granted man a certain lifetime and waits for them to be tested (Surely God is beyond all that). And He will wait until the end of the universe. Yet, this is surely impossible. Waiting is a weakness peculiar to man and God is surely not bound by such weakness. God's attribute, the al-Quddus (The Holy), with which God presents Himself to us in the Qur'an, means "free from all error, incapability and from any kind of defect". That is why God knows the past and future of all people, as well as their experiences, in great detail. But man, in this life, the arena of this test, assumes time to be linear with a beginning and an end. Yet, as stated earlier in this section, it is not possible to talk of the concepts of past and present. Everything, all people, all living beings live **simultaneously**. All ages, minutes, seconds and even all days, hours and moments occur at the same time. Though man is unable to see this due to the limited capacity of his sensations, this fact is evident. In the section "Relativity of the Qur'an", many examples were given to explain the difference between the time man is bound by and time in the sight of God. God draws our attention to this issue in the following verse:

Truly, a day in the sight of your Lord is like a thousand years of your reckoning. (Surat Al-Hajj: 47)

God, the al-Hasib, knows in detail the account of things people do throughout their lives. If one remembers that nothing that is experienced and that exists ever disappears, one will have a better grasp of this attribute of God. That God knows everything, every detail of every event that is experienced is stressed in the following verse:

> Truly, God alone has knowledge of the Hour of Doom. It is He Who sends down rain, and He Who knows what every womb contains. No self knows what he will earn tomorrow: nor does anyone know in what land he is to die. Truly, God has full knowledge of all things. (Surah Luqman: 34)

This is the main reason why believers appreciate the glory of God, submit to Him and put their trust in Him. His Majesty simply reminds one how prone one is to weakness and how one is in need of Him. They are aware how weak they are next to His might. This superior moral attribute displayed by believers is referred to in the Qur'an:

> Say: "Nothing will happen to us except what God has decreed for us: He is our protector": and in God alone should believers put their trust. (Surat at-Tawbah: 51)

> Say: "I possess no power to harm or help myself except as God wills." (Surah Yunus: 49)

People whose faith is assured and who say these words are the ones who can conceive of God's attributes. That is why they wholeheartedly submit to God.

Death is Not Extinction

Death is also one of the issues about which people have misconceptions. Someone who dies is regarded as simply perishing. Because they have inadequate information regarding the hereafter, the eternal life, paradise and hell, people commonly either never believe in resurrection after death or harbour vague convictions about it. Consequently, the majority surmise they lose someone for ever when he or she dies. This is surely a completely bigoted stance. By the time one is born (once he is brought into the realm of existence by God), one's eternal life has begun. Like all other moments composing one's lifetime, death is merely a single moment that one experiences, but, in reality, that person is still alive. All moments before and after death and everything pertaining to one's life are preserved without changing. For instance, after the death of someone people mourn and say, "It is unfortunate that he died; he was so young." However, all the details of one's life, memories of childhood, birth and family still exist. They do not fade or become extinct. All experiences are preserved. As a requisite of the test in this world, these memories are simply wiped from one's memory; however, this, is by no means, the equivalent of their not existing.

In the sight of God, the birth, life and death of a man take place and finish simultaneously. The same reasoning applies to all human beings. All human beings are coming into existence and dying right at this moment. All are being resurrected and being sent to paradise or hell. Thus, no one dies and nobody is reduced to insignificance; all individuals are alive for all eternity. Within eternity, man spends only a portion of his time in the world, and during this period where he is doomed to go— either paradise or hell— is known. Just at this moment, some of the people currently living in this world are in paradise while others are in hell. This fact is stressed in the Qur'an; in many verses relating to paradise and hell, the life in the hereafter is referred to in the simple present or past tense, which draws one's attention to the fact that all these incidents are taking place at a single moment:

> Truly, the Companions of the Garden that Day have joy in all that they do; they and their associates are in shady groves, reclining on Thrones (of dignity). (Surah Ya sin: 55-56)

> And those who feared their Lord were led to the Garden in crowds: until behold, they arrived there; its gates were opened; and its keepers said: "Peace be upon you! You have led good lives! Enter Paradise and dwell in it forever." They said: "Praise be to God, Who has truly fulfilled His Promise to us, and has given us this land as a heritage: We can dwell in the Garden as we will: how excellent a reward for the righteous!" And you see the angels surrounding the Divine Throne on all sides, glorifying

their Lord with praise. They are judged with fairness and all say: "Praise be to God, the Lord of the Worlds!" (Surat az-Zumar: 73-75)

And the sinful saw the fire and realised they are going to fall into it and find no way of escaping from it. (Surat al-Kahf: 53)

In human life, another important mystery prevails. While mourning for someone who has died, people do not consider that they, themselves, have also died and even been resurrected. The birth and death of a person occur simultaneously. Even trivial details about all people's lives, deaths, resurrections and eternal lives are retained in the sight of God. In other words, everything is taking place right at this moment. Death and resurrection are truly not incidents occurring at distinct times.

People are born in timelessness. Likewise, they die in timelessness, they are resurrected in timelessness and, as a matter of fact, just at this moment, they are alive. By the moment God creates man, he becomes an eternal being. To put it another way, he starts his endless life, becoming alive for all eternity. Meanwhile, he also witnesses his own death as a single square. Just as he sees himself alive all through his life, he witnesses his death, but only on one occasion.

An example will further clarify this subject. In the Qur'an, God informs us that sleep is also created as a form of death. Thus, every night one witnesses his death when he goes to sleep and witnesses his resurrection when he wakes up in the morning. This fact is manifested in the following verse:

God takes back people's selves when their death arrives and those who have not yet died, while they are asleep. He keeps hold of those whose death has been decreed and sends the others back for a specified term. There are certainly Signs in that for people who reflect. (Surat az-Zumar: 42)

Hence, man unceasingly witnesses his death and resurrection all through his life. Similarly, he will also see his real death. Consequently, his birth, death and resurrection as well as his eternal abode are all known and man is forever alive in the sight of God. All these incidents have taken place and finished in the sight of God. That is why, death, in the sense that it is commonly understood, is not a termination or extinction.

Considering these facts, mourning for someone who dies and feeling sorry for his death sound simply irrational. A young man, a child or a healthy person who dies does not, after all, perish; each exists in his best state. In the sight of God, each is alive. This is a clear indication of God's greatness, which is also stated in the Qur'an:

> God, there is no deity except Him, the Living, the Self-Sustaining. He is not subject to drowsiness or sleep. Everything in the heavens and the earth belongs to Him. Who can intercede with Him except by His permission? He knows what is before them and what is behind them but they cannot grasp any of His knowledge save what He wills. His Footstool encompasses the heavens and the earth and their preservation does not tire Him. He is the Most High, the Magnificent. (Surat al-Baqarah: 255)

The Life of an Animal Is Also A Single Moment

By the time life came into existence on earth, all phases an animal went through had been retained in the sight of God. For instance, the birth, death, the first hunt of a penguin, which lived at the south pole and died 250 years ago, exist currently in the sight of God and will continue to exist forever. By the same token, all these incidents are happening just at this moment.

Every moment of a pet an animal lover possessed in his childhood remains in the sight of God. The moment he played with it, the moment he caressed it, the moment it died in an accident, in brief, each moment whether he remembers it or not...

This also holds true for animals we never saw. A camel, which lived and died 700 years ago, a crocodile in the Amazon in 5 BC, a snake that will crack the shell of its egg in the year 2200, or a kangaroo in Australia today. As a matter of fact, all these details and incidents pertaining to the animals mentioned above, as well as of all other animals of all times, occur simultaneously, that is to say, right at this moment. Every

The butterflies and flowers, in short, all the details you see in a garden which you pass by are preserved in the sight of God.

moment of this camel, including the moment it was born, the moment it carried a load in the desert and the moment it drank water are all retained in the sight of God. Just now, the camel in question, however, is still drinking water, and is still carrying its load… All the camels that have ever lived throughout world history and each moment they spent in this world are still alive.

This may seem to be beyond the grasp of the human mind, when one considers that there have been trillions of animals living on the planet. Yet, a mystery of the might of God is hidden here. God, the al-Alim, is the All-Knowing. God surely knows everything about each being, whether it is living, inanimate or dead. This remarkable fact is related in the following verse:

> **He does take an account of them (all), and has numbered them (all) exactly. (Surah Maryam: 94)**

The death of animals is no different from that of human beings. As is the case with human beings, the moments of an animal's life do not vanish after its death either. At the sudden death of one's pet, —for instance,

a bird,— one feels sorry. That bird, however, is not dead; it is retained in
the memory of God in its best state. The time this bird spent in its egg, the
day it came one's house and the time it struggled to fly as a young bird
are entirely in the memory of God. Alternatively, in the sight of God, each
moment of a dead dog's past life and the moment it died are known. All
moments pertaining to the dog's past life; while it was still a puppy, while
it barked, walked, drank water and all its other states unknown to its
owner are available in the sight of God.

The same reasoning applies to all animals. The birth and death of the
dog mentioned in Surat al-Kahf, and each moment it spent in front of the
cave is in the memory of God. Likewise, the camel brought by the Prophet
Salih, and the moment his people slew the camel, though clearly prohib-
ited by God, are in His memory. Alternatively, the moment a beast is
killed by being trodden upon remains in the sight of God. The death of the
beast lasts only a moment and, like all other beings, it is only an image
and each image of it remains in the sight of God. That we do not see anything pertaining to the beast after it has died does not mean that it disappears. The death of an insect is also over in a single moment. Like all other
beings, it is only a perception for us and every image regarding its life
remains without changing. That we do not see anything connected with it
does not mean that it has disappeared. It has merely vanished from one's
memory. In the sight of God, if the image belonging to that insect is ani-
mated again, and presented to our five senses, we may see it again.

The same is true of a colourful butterfly seen by a man during the
period of the French Revolution. It is quite possible that the man felt sorry
for this beautiful butterfly when he saw that it had become a prey for a
bird. However, that butterfly, with all its symmetric beauty and colours, is
right now in the sight of God. Every moment of the butterfly, every time
it opened its wings, every time it closed them, every flower it visited are
known in the sight of God. Furthermore, this butterfly is doing all these
deeds just now. Just now, this butterfly is flying, right now it is eating and
right now, it is dying... After all, this butterfly is alive, and it will remain
alive for all eternity. The feelings of the man who felt sorry for the death

of this butterfly, and moreover, each and every moment of this man's life exist forever.

This fact is stressed in the following verse:

Certainly there is no hidden thing in either heaven or earth which is not in a Clear Book. (Surat an-Naml: 75)

These explanations provide explicit answers to some frequently asked questions, such as, "Do animals have a spirit?" or "What will be their end?" These living beings are in the memory of God and this is the point that really matters. As long as the information about any animal is recorded in the sight of God (remember that by the time it is created, it is destined to eternity), it is alive. Yet, what is meant by "alive" here is God's creating it in the form of a sensation. In this sense, none of the other living beings bear any similarity to God's attribute, the al-Hayy (The Ever-Living). In that sense, the really important thing is not whether the animal has a spirit or not, but whether it is created in the memory or not. If God wills, this living being exists in our memory; if not, it does not. If God takes back the image of an animal from one's memory, this means that it has died. If, however, He gives it back to the memory, this means that it has become alive. It must be borne in mind that this animal remains in the memory of God forever, since God is not bound by time. In timelessness, it is not possible to talk of past, present and future. It is all a single moment.

Flowers Never Fade, Fruits Never Disappear...

God is the One Who retains the knowledge of everything. As stated in the verse above, since the creation of the universe, all the leaves, and the different states they go through during their life span, are all known by God. For instance, the information about a tree which grew in Babylon — down to a single leaf of this tree, is all kept in the sight of God. Furthermore, all stages of this leaf pertaining to its fall from the tree are individually kept in the memory of God. Sitting under this tree in Babylon, a man watching the leaf falling, too, unknowingly remains there. None of the seconds he spent in watching this leaf disappeared or remained in the past.

Most probably, the fall of a single leaf from a tree might be perceived as an insignificant incident. Nevertheless, the fall of all the leaves which have ever existed throughout history is also in the memory of God.

In one of the verses, this fact is related as follows:

...He knows everything in the land and sea. No leaf falls without His knowing it. There is no seed in the darkness of the earth, and nothing moist or dry which is not in a Clear Book. (Surat al-An'am: 59)

The only thing one who comprehends this fact should do is to submit himself to his Creator.

As stated in the verse, **"He rules all affairs from the heavens to the earth..."** (Surat as-Sajdah: 5), all animals, plants, human beings, in brief, all living beings and events are created by God and their information is kept in the sight of God.

The same facts also hold true for flowers. Contrary to the common belief, a poppy does not disappear when it fades: it simply continues to exist in the sight of God. As made clear in the verse **"For He is Well-versed in every kind of creation!"** (Surah Ya sin: 79), all phases of the flower; its budding, as well as this very same flower in bloom, together with its faded state, are all present. Besides, as stated earlier, the consecutive changes occurring in the

The consecutive changes occurring in a flower, though seemingly taking place at distinct times, are actually taking place simultaneously. After a while, the different images in the memory of a person who sees this flower disappear. Yet, every moment remains in the eternal memory of God.

poppy, though seemingly separate, are in fact phases occurring **simultaneously**. In the sight of God, all details pertaining to a single poppy are kept. However, God makes this information known to whomever He wills. In the memory of those who see the poppy, all the images relating to it disappear. Yet, every image remains forever in the memory of God.

God, the al-Muhsi (The Counter), Who knows the number of all things although they cannot be counted, knows the number of every leaf falling. Besides, all plants, leaves and flowers, all moments from their birth to death, their growth, drying and falling, as well as each rain drop falling on them are within the knowledge of God. These, with all the moments of all other living beings, are created in a single moment and on a single plane. As a whole, they are brought into being right **now**. Consequently, when a leaf dries and falls down, this does not mean that it is dead; it is only erased from our memory. However, they may still be alive in someone else's memory. If God presents its image to someone else's memory, he continues to see this particular leaf.

The same is true of a violet in your flowerpot. The budding stage of your violet, the first moment it faded and fell down to the ground are all in the sight of God. In other words, the violet is blossoming right at this

The concept of time is valid only for man. The memory of God is above all times. Throughout history, all violets, which existed, are actually blossoming right now, just as they are fading now. The same is also true for the violets you grow in your flowerpot.

moment. Yet, it is also fading just at this moment. There is no time gap between its blossoming and its fading. The time concept exists only for us; the memory of God is superior to all times. Remembering this fact, one realises that all violets, which existed all through history, are blossoming **simultaneously**, just as how they are fading **at the same time**. All the moments of the lifetime of a tiny little plant in an African jungle which grew 1500 years ago are also coded in the "The Mother of the Book". Similarly, 14 centuries ago, the tree under which true believers swore allegiance to our Prophet Muhammad, the production of seeds by this tree, extension of its buds, as well as the drying up of this tree, take place right at this moment. All the moments of a blade of grass, growing on any mountain of the earth, a cactus in any desert, a bush growing in a remote part of the world, a snowdrop in the tundra or a daisy growing near a motorway are all kept in the memory of God. Most probably, no one on earth is aware of these plants and from now on, no one will ever recognise them. However, they are all known to God:

... Whom not even the weight of smallest particle eludes, either in the heavens or in the earth; nor is there anything smaller or larger than that which is not in a Clear Book. (Surah Saba': 3)

Knowledge of the Hour is referred to Him. And no fruit emerges from its husk, nor does any female get pregnant or give birth, without His knowledge. (Surah Fussilat: 47)

In another verse, the same fact is stressed as follows:

He knows what goes into the earth and what comes out of it, and what comes down from heaven and what goes up into it. And He is the Most Merciful, the Ever-Forgiving. (Surah Saba': 2)

To have a better grasp of these explanations, one can think about fruits. The taste, odour, colour, and ripeness of a banana growing in Africa is in the sight of God. Even before the seed of this banana tree is planted in the soil, the moment the banana is plucked from its branch, the person plucking it and the time this banana will be eaten are known by God. God informs us about this fact in the following verse:

There is no creature on the earth which is not dependent upon God for its provision. He knows where it lives and where it dies. They are all in a Clear Book. (Surah Hud: 6)

Every stage the banana goes through from the moment it is plucked till it is eaten, is in the memory of God. It may seem that a long period of time passed between when the banana flower first blossomed on its branch and the moment it was eaten. In other words, one might assume that the banana existed for a considerably long time. This fruit became ripe, and then it was plucked from its branch. Then it went through several stages like packaging, loading, shipment, storing, distribution, deliv-

Every stage of the formation of raindrops is within the knowledge of God. God is Well-versed in every kind of creation.

ery, and lastly purchasing. Most probably a member of the family of the person who bought this banana or a visitor will eat it. Yet, as stressed earlier in former sections, this sequence of events is perceived by man, a being bound by time and space. In the sight of God, however, the whole life of the banana takes place at a single moment. The banana is growing right **at this moment** and is being eaten again **at this moment**. Yet, the same banana is being plucked from its branch, just as it is being loaded on to a truck right **now**.

To repeat, the life of that banana, or your life, as well as the life of Julius Caesar, Alexander the Great or of Edison, is lived **in the same moment.** The knowledge of all fruits, plants, human beings and animals, ever to have lived throughout history, is in the memory of God. These

All details, such as what will happen as these trees are cut down, who will cut them down, in the construction of which house they will be used, are determined beforehand in the sight of God.

facts are surely comprehensible for those who ponder deeply and with sincerity.

Another important point is that none of these fruits decay, disappear or become extinct. Think of an orange that grew in a Mediterranean country 50 years ago. Many details regarding this orange are predestined; such as when it will grow and on which tree, whether it will be sour or sweet, its shape, its exact colour, the place where it will be stored, the truck by which it will be transported, the grocery shop in which it will be sold, the customer who will buy it…Maybe it will be forgotten in a fruit basket. In this case, the process through which it goes totally mouldy, the moment it is found by someone and thrown into the trash are all predestined. As we have seen, every second of even an orange's life, the first moment it buds, ripens or decays exists in the sight of God for all eternity. Therefore, that orange does not vanish in the sight of God. That is because, God is the al-Hayy. In other words, He is alive. Everything in His memory becomes alive from His saying "BE!".

> It is He Who sends down water from the sky from which We bring forth plants of every kind, and from that We bring forth the green shoots and from them We bring

Every second of the life span of a single orange is preserved in the memory of God for all eternity.

forth close-packed seeds, and from the spathes of the date palm date clusters hanging down, and gardens of grapes and olives and pomegranates, both similar and dissimilar. Look at their fruits as they bear fruit and ripen. There are Signs in that for people who have faith. (Surat al-An'am: 99)

Not A Drop of Water Disappears

What has been related so far is also valid for running water. Each drop of a stream, a spring, a fountain, an artesian well, or a fall is kept in the sight of God. Not a drop disappears and is wasted. It continues to exist for all eternity. As is the case with living beings, all moments and states pertaining to them are hidden in God's memory. All waters which have run ever since the beginning of the universe, the ones currently running, as well as the ones which will run in the future are actually running just **at this moment.** That is to say, all are running **at this single moment.** There is a time in eternity and all incidents take place in one moment.

The water which ran 300 years ago in the Mississippi, and the water which ran 500 years ago in the Rhine as well as the water which will run in 200 years time in the River Euphrates are, in reality, running simultaneously in a single moment. They are all running **at this very moment.** Not a drop of water disappears; it continues to run forever in the sight of God.

Waters all over the universe are also running at a single moment. Even a drop of water does not disappear; it is preserved in the sight of God for all eternity.

Going Back To The Beginning is Also Possible

That everything is in the memory of God brings us to another important mystery: by the will of God, going back to the initial moment of an event is also possible. Being bound by time, such an incident seems impossible for man. Yet, in the sight of God, time does not exist. As stressed earlier, past and present are all a single moment; just as a videotape cassette includes all the actions moment by moment. After watching a film, it is possible to rewind and re-watch it. Likewise, the same is true for daily events; by the will of God, it is possible to see past events again. It is surely easy for God to recreate a past event.

An example will contribute to a fuller understanding of these facts: The gardens of Saba' that have been converted into **"gardens containing bitter-tasting plants and tamarisk and a few lote trees"** (Surah Saba': 16),

The states in which these areas were 1000 years ago or 500 years ago together with the foundations, which will be built on in the future, actually exist at a single moment.

as referred to in the Qur'an, are still in the sight of God. The state of the garden both before and after its destruction remains in the memory of God. Thousands of years ago, in a remote part of the world, the transformation of a beautiful garden into a wheat field is in the sight of God. A house built on this wheat field after hundreds of years, as well as the collapse of this building and construction of a workshop in its place are all present in the sight of God. Finally, the current state of this wheat field, now a region populated with ghettos, is also present in the sight of God. All the intermediary stages in between these views of the same area, too, are in the sight of God for all eternity. By the will of God, it is possible to go back and see the initial appearance of this garden.

Surely, all beings and incidents that have existed since the beginning of the universe are in the memory of God. None of these moments are missing. This is indeed a remarkable phenomenon. This fact is a great blessing for believers in paradise, since they might wish to see their past life or certain historical events. By the will of God, believers might actually have the opportunity to see these events.

For instance, one might wish to see the big-bang, the first moment of the creation of the universe, the initial formation of galaxies, the initial stages of the first atom, the phases one goes through in one's mother's womb, a war which took place in ancient times, the lives of living beings in the depths of oceans, the sinking of the Titanic, the childhood of one's mother, the life of one's grandson, a cat lost years ago or a plant planted in childhood. All these events, with all their details are present in the sight of God. In this sense, by the will of God, man has the chance to see whatever he wishes, which is surely of great blessing to him.

The Responsibility This Information Imposes On Man

The subjects which have been related so far are surely very important and striking. The aspect of this issue which is crucial for us is the following: every moment we live, every attitude we assume, every word we utter or every thought we harbour are kept in the sight of God. That believers are aware of this fact is manifested in the words of the Prophet Jesus, in the following verse:

> And when God says, "'Jesus son of Mary! Did you say to people, 'Take me and my mother as two gods instead of God alone?'" he will say, "Glory be to You! It is not for me to say what I have no right to say! If I had said it, then You would have known it. You know what is in my self but I do not know what is in Your Self. You are the Knower of all unseen things." (Surat al-Ma'idah: 116)

Messengers before you were mocked. I gave those who disbelieve a little more time and then I seized them. How terrible was my retribution! (Surat ar-Ra'd: 32)

There is another aspect of this fact: any attitude, which is not favoured by God, or any deed, which is not within the limits of God, are all kept in the memory of God. Anyone trying to deny any misdeeds will fail, since he will see the images relative to these misdeeds. Since nothing disappears, misdeeds are also retained. Therefore, those failing to observe the limits of God or engaging in deeds which will not earn the good pleasure of God - assuming that nobody sees or hears them - will be greatly astonished. They will individually witness that God knows everything:

> He is God in the heavens and in the earth. He knows what you keep secret and what you make public and He knows what you earn. (Surat al-An'am: 3)

However, on Judgment Day, the day when everyone will see his deeds, nobody will have any opportunity to save himself since, as stressed by God in the Qur'an, on that day God will encompass them entirely:

> ... What confronts them from God will be something they did not reckon with. What confronts them will be the evil actions which they earned and what they used to mock at will engulf them. (Surat az-Zumar: 47-48)

The Day of Judgement will be the day unbelievers will face something they never expected to face: God will disclose all the misdeeds the unbelievers try to hide. Just as stated in the verse, what unbelievers used to mock at all through their lives will, this time, engulf them. The faith of believers in God and the hereafter had always been an issue ridiculed by unbelievers all throughout their lives. They merely interpret these certified facts as misconceptions. To their disappointment, however, these facts encompass them all in an unexpected way, since they themselves have been deceived. All their misdeeds are present in the memory of God and on the Day of Judgment, they will come face to face with each one of them. Every time they try to deny them, the images pertaining to their misdeeds will be presented to them. This will be the time they will realise that the knowledge of God surrounds them all. God describes this state of the unbelievers as follows:

> God is mocking them, and drawing them on, as they wander blindly in their excessive insolence. (Surat al-Baqarah: 15)

Without exception, the violence resorted to by unbelievers in the time of the Prophet Muhammad, the misdeeds perpetrated by unbelievers in the respective periods of the Prophets Noah and Abraham are all kept in the sight of God. That the Prophet Joseph (Yusuf) was thrown down to the bottom of the well by his brothers or that the people of Israel mistreated the Prophet Moses are, by no means, forgotten; with no exception, they all exist in the sight of God. Everything, most probably with all the details no one has ever witnessed before, is kept in its entirety. This fact is stressed in the following verse:

> They may try to hide from people while they can never hide from God. He is with them when they spend the night saying things which are not pleasing to Him. God encompasses everything they do. (Surat an-Nisa': 108)

The same thing holds true for those unbelievers living in our day. They confidently assume that the plots they plan against believers or religion will remain hidden and they will never have to face them on the Day of Judgment. But the slightest wicked deed, and every slander they make up against believers are in the memory of God. The fact that these images are withdrawn from their memory should not deceive them. It may be quite possible that they themselves forgot a slander they spread about believers a decade ago. However, all these misdeeds exist in the memory of God. By the Will of God, these incidents might, at any time, reappear in their memories. Yet, unaware of this fact, and **"because they are a people without understanding"** (Surat al-Ma'idah: 58), unbelievers cannot comprehend the might of God. Yet, on the Day of Judgment, they will see the reality and suffer great shame and regret.

The response of the Prophet Shu'ayb to such an attitude on the part of the leaders of his people draws our attention to the same point — that they are people without understanding:

> They said, "Shu'ayb, We do not understand much of what you say and we see you are weak among us. Were it not for your immediate family, we would have stoned you. We do not hold you in high esteem!" He said, "My people! Do you esteem my family ties more than you do God? You have made Him into something to cast disdainfully behind your backs! But my Lord encompasses everything that you do!" (Surah Hud: 91-92)

When God creates the Day of Judgment, He will be very swift at reckoning the unbelievers. When one fully comprehends the facts presented throughout the book - that every moment of everything that is created is preserved for all eternity - it will surely not be difficult to imagine that all people will be judged very swiftly, in a single moment. Moreover, it is essential that one should not consider this moment very far off, because that moment is actually now. In other words, all people are giving an account of the misdeeds they have committed in this world right now. Unbelievers imagine that what they do will not be seen or heard, or will be forgotten. However, on the Day of Judgment they will be greatly disappointed:

> You thought that God did not know many of the things that you used to do! "But this thought of yours which you entertained about your Lord, has brought you to destruction, so that now you are among the utterly lost!" (Surah Fussilat: 22-23)

Conclusion

*T*he foregoing exposition should have given the reader a clearer conception of the fact that God encompasses everything. In timelessness and in a world of a collection of images, man is being tested all alone by his Creator. This leaves man all alone with God. The verse, **"Leave Me alone, to deal with the creature whom I created bare and alone."** (Surat Al-Muddaththir: 11) is a clear indication of this truth.

Once in possession of the facts explained in this book, the reader will easily comprehend that including himself, man lives in a world comprised merely of sensations. In this universe of perceptions, the sole absolute being is God. There is no other deity but Him. All the things people attach importance to and hence cast their religion away for are simply meaningless:

> That is because God – He is the Truth, and what you call upon besides Him is falsehood. God is the All-High, the Most Great. (Surah Luqman: 30)

On a three-dimensional, high quality screen, an individual watches a film being projected. Since he is almost attached to this screen, he cannot succeed in detaching himself from it, so that he may grasp the situation he is in. Forgetting that he is in the presence of God and is being tested by Him, he feels himself to be an independent and separate being, apart from God. Hence, he assumes himself to be very important. His experiences in life seem to be so real that he considers his imaginary body, his imaginary possessions, his imaginary family, and imaginary friends he watches on the screen to be real and feels pride in them. However, as it is stated expressly in the verse, **"Blessed be Him to whom belongs the sovereignty of the heavens and the earth and everything in between them.."** (Surat az-Zukhruf: 85), the sole owner of these possessions is God. Were God to withdraw this image from the screen, even for a moment, the human watcher would recognise that he is all alone. Furthermore, he would feel ashamed of being proud of all the images he watches on the screen; that is to say, of his body, his possessions and everything else he sees in the external world.

A sensate being pondering over these facts would also appreciate his weakness in the sight of God. He can earn esteem and lead a pleasurable life for all eternity only when he bows to his Creator. Only then can he hope for God to show him the images of paradise for all eternity. That is because, just as this world is a collection of perceptions, so are paradise and hell. All images pertaining to paradise and hell are preserved in the memory of God. And God allows those He wills to see these images.

What God expects from His servants is quite explicit: to appreciate His power and to lead a life observing His limits. Yet, some people, because of their heedlessness, forget their Creator or deny Him. At this point, one of the major factors misleading them is the crowd of people, — which they assume to exist — surrounding them. These people display such a rebellious attitude because they assume their friends, associates, everyone who shares the same mentality with them, exist, and because they forget that they are all alone. To their disappointment, however, each one of them is all alone, no matter with how many people he is surrounded. There is no one to help him except for God:

> ...They will not find any protector or helper for themselves besides God. (Surat an-Nisa': 173)

As stressed in the verse **"Each of them will come to Him on the Day of Resurrection, alone."** (Surah Maryam: 95), on the Day of Judgement, they will be all alone in the presence of God. Nor will their friends and relatives, who forget the Day of Judgment and hereafter, be next to them on that Day. And certainly satan, whom they followed eagerly, will leave them:

> He led me astray from the Reminder after it came to me. The evil always leaves man in the lurch. (Surat al-Furqan: 29)

> You have come to Us all alone just as We created you at first, leaving behind you everything We bestowed on you. We do not see your intercessors accompanying you, those you claimed were your partners with God. The link between you is cut. Those you made such claims for have forsaken you. (Surat al-An'am: 94)

For those having a sincere approach, it is easy to grasp these facts. The explanations in the Qur'an are quite explicit. This fact never changes, whether you are in the middle of a crowd, in a cinema, in a meeting, in a busy street, or among your close friends. You are, in reality, all alone. The state of those who cannot grasp this fact due to their prejudiced attitude is explained in the following verse:

...that is because they are a people devoid of wisdom. (Surat al-Hashr: 14)

Those who set aside their prejudice and ponder over these facts are the believers, those who can think and take heed:

Is one who worships devoutly during the night, prostrating himself or standing in adoration, who takes heed of the Hereafter, and who places his hope in the Mercy of his Lord like one who does not? Say: "Are those equal, those who know and those who do not know? Truly, none will take heed but men of understanding." (Surat az-Zumar: 9)

Is then one who knows that what has been revealed to you by your Lord is the Truth, like one who is blind? Truly, none will take heed but the wise. (Surat az-Zumar: 19)

So, you also submit to God and obey Him.

And avoid being, as is said in the verse, "the one who is blind."

The Evolution Deceit

very detail in this universe points to a superior creation. On the contrary, materialism, which seeks to deny the fact of creation in the universe, is nothing but an unscientific fallacy.

With materialism invalidated, all other theories based on this philosophy are rendered baseless. The foremost of them is Darwinism, that is, the theory of evolution. This theory, which argues that life originated from inanimate matter through coincidences, has been demolished with the recognition of the fact that the universe was created by God. American astrophysicist Hugh Ross explains this as follows:

> Atheism, Darwinism, and virtually all the "isms" emanating from the eighteenth to the twentieth century philosophies are built upon the assumption, the incorrect assumption, that the universe is infinite. The singularity has brought us face to face with the cause – or causer – beyond/behind/before the universe and all that it contains, including life itself.[30]

It is God Who created the universe and who designed it down to its smallest detail. Therefore, it is impossible for the theory of evolution, which holds that living beings were not created by God, but are products of coincidences, to be true.

Unsurprisingly, when we look at the theory of evolution, we see that this theory is denounced by scientific findings. The design in life is extremely complex and striking. In the inanimate world, for instance, we can explore how sensitive are the balances which atoms rest upon, and further, in the animate world, we can observe in how complex designs these atoms were brought together, and how extraordinary as mechanisms are structures such as proteins, enzymes, and cells, which are manufactured from them.

This extraordinary design in life invalidated Darwinism at the end of the 20th century.

We dealt with this subject in great detail in some of our other studies, and we still do. However, we think that, due to its importance, it will be helpful to make a short summary here as well.

The Scientific Collapse of Darwinism

Although a doctrine going back as far as ancient Greece, the theory of evolution was not advanced extensively until the 19th century. The most important development that made this theory the most compelling topic of the world of science was the publication in 1859 of Charles Darwin's book titled "The Origin of Species." In this book, Darwin denied that different living species on the earth were created separately by God. According to Darwin, all living beings had a common ancestor and they diversified over time through small changes.

Darwin's theory was not based on any concrete scientific finding; as he also accepted, it was just an "assumption." Moreover, as Darwin confessed in the long chapter of his book titled "Difficulties of the Theory," the theory was failing in the face of many critical questions.

Darwin invested all his hopes in new scientific discoveries, which he expected to solve the "Difficulties of the Theory." However, contrary to his expectations, scientific findings expanded the dimensions of these difficulties.

The defeat of Darwinism against science can be reviewed under three basic headings:

1) The theory can by no means explain how life originated on the earth.

2) There is no scientific finding showing that the "evolutionary mechanisms" proposed by the theory have any power to evolve at all.

3) The fossil record proves quite the contrary of the suggestions of the theory of evolution.

In this section, we will examine these three basic points in general outline:

Charles Darwin

The First Insurmountable Step:
The Origin of Life

The theory of evolution posits that all living species evolved from a single living cell that emerged on the primitive earth 3.8 billion years ago. How a single cell could generate millions of complex living species and if such an evolution really occurred, why traces of it cannot be observed in the fossil record are some questions the theory cannot answer. However, first and foremost, the first step of the alleged evolutionary process has to be inquired into. How did this "first cell" originate?

Since the theory of evolution denies creation and does not accept any kind of supernatural intervention, it maintains that the "first cell" originated coincidentally within laws of nature, without any design, plan, or arrangement. According to the theory, inanimate matter must have produced a living cell as a result of coincidences. This, however, is a claim inconsistent with the most clearly recognized rules of biology.

"Life Comes from Life"

In his book, Darwin never referred to the origin of life. The primitive understanding of science in his time rested on the assumption that living beings had a very simple structure. Since medieval times, spontaneous generation, the theory asserting that non-living materials came together to form living organisms, was widely accepted. It was commonly believed that insects came into being from food leftovers, and mice from wheat. Interesting experiments were conducted to prove this theory. Some wheat was placed on a dirty piece of cloth, and it was believed that mice would originate out of it after a while.

Similarly, worming of meat was assumed to be an evidence for spontaneous generation. However, only some time later was it understood that worms did not appear on meat spontaneously, but were carried to it by flies in the form of larvae, invisible to the naked eye.

Even in the period when Darwin wrote The Origin of Species, the belief that bacteria could come into existence from non-living matter was widely accepted in the world of science.

However, five years after Darwin's book was published, the discovery of Louis Pasteur disproved this belief, which constituted the groundwork of evolution. Pasteur summarized the conclusion he reached after time-consuming studies and experiments: "The claim that inanimate matter can originate life is buried in history for good."[31]

With the experiments he carried out, Louis Pasteur invalidated the claim that "inanimate matter can create life", which constituted the groundwork of the theory of evolution.

Advocates of the theory of evolution resisted the findings of Pasteur for a long time. However, as the development of science unraveled the complex structure of the cell of a living being, the idea that life could come into being coincidentally faced an even greater impasse.

Inconclusive Efforts in the 20th Century

The first evolutionist who took up the subject of the origin of life in the 20th century was the renowned Russian biologist, Alexander Oparin. With various theses he advanced in the 1930's, he tried to prove that the cell of a living being could originate by coincidence. These studies, however, were doomed to failure, and Oparin had to make the following confession: "Unfortunately, the origin of the cell remains a question which is actual-

Alexander Oparin's attempts to offer an evolutionist explanation for the origin of life ended in a great fiasco.

ly the darkest point of the complete evolution theory."[32]

Evolutionist followers of Oparin tried to carry out experiments to clear up the enigma of the origin of life. The best known of these experiments was carried out by American chemist Stanley Miller in 1953. Combining in an experiment the gases he alleged to have existed in the primordial earth atmosphere and adding energy to the mixture, Miller synthesized several organic molecules (amino acids) present in the structure of proteins.

It only took a few years for it to be revealed that this experiment, which was

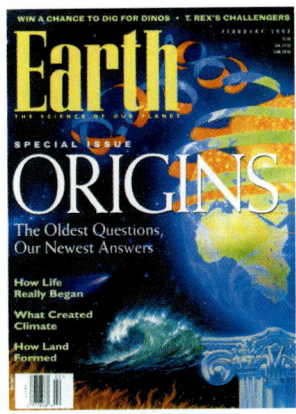

As accepted also by the latest evolutionist theorists, the origin of life is still a great stumbling block for the theory of evolution.

then presented as an important step in the name of evolution, was invalid, and that the atmosphere used in the experiment was very different from that of real earth conditions.[33]

After a long silence, Miller confessed that the atmosphere medium he used was unrealistic.[34]

All the evolutionist efforts throughout the 20th century which were meant to explain the origin of life ended in failure. The geochemist Jeffrey Bada from San Diego Scripps Institute accepts this fact in an article published in *Earth* Magazine in 1998:

> Today, as we leave the twentieth century, we still face the biggest unsolved problem that we had when we entered the twentieth century: How did life originate on Earth?[35]

The Complex Structure of Life

The primary reason why the theory of the evolutionary origin of life ended up in a major impasse is that even the living organisms deemed the simplest have incredibly complex structures. The cell of a living being is more complex than all of the technological products produced by man. Today, even in the most developed laboratories in the world, a living cell cannot be produced by bringing inorganic materials together.

The conditions required for the formation of a cell are too great in quantity to be explained away by coincidences. The probability of proteins, the building blocks of the cell, being synthesized coincidentally, is 1 in 10^{950} for an average protein made up of 500 amino acids. In mathematics, a probability smaller than 1 over 10^{50} is practically considered to be impossible.

The DNA molecule, which is located in the nucleus of the cell and which stores genetic information, is an incredible databank. It is calculated that if the information coded in DNA were written down, this would make a giant library consisting of 900 volumes of encyclopedias of 500 pages each.

A very interesting dilemma emerges at this point: the DNA can replicate only with the help of some specialized proteins (enzymes). However, the synthesis of these enzymes can be realized only by using the information coded in DNA. As they both depend on each other, they have to exist at the same time for replication. This brings the scenario that life originated by itself to a deadlock. Reputable evolutionist Prof. Leslie Orgel from the University of San Diego California, admits to this fact in the September 1994 issue of the *Scientific American* magazine:

> It is extremely improbable that proteins and nucleic acids, both of which are structurally complex, arose spontaneously in the same place at the same time. Yet it also seems impossible to have one without the other. And so, at first glance, one might have to conclude that life could never, in fact, have originated by chemical means.[36]

No doubt, if it is impossible for life to have originated by natural causes, then it has to be accepted that life is "created" in a supernatural way. This fact explicitly invalidates the theory of evolution, whose main purpose is to deny creation.

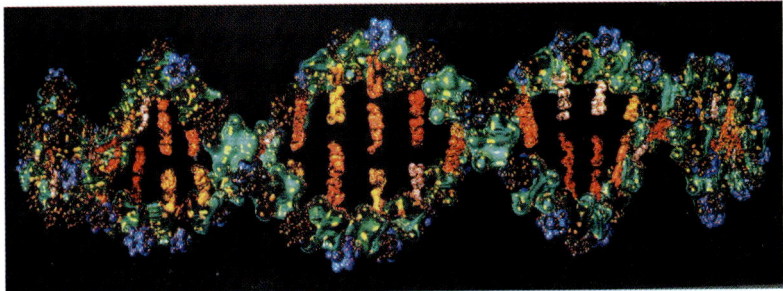

One of the facts nullifying the theory of evolution is the incredibly complex structure of life. The DNA molecule located in the nucleus of cells of living beings is an example of this. The DNA is a sort of databank formed of the arrangement of four different molecules in different sequences. This databank contains the codes of all the physical traits of that living being. When the human DNA is put into writing, it is calculated that this would result in an encyclopaedia made up of 900 volumes. Unquestionably, such extraordinary information definitely refutes the concept of coincidence.

Imaginary Mechanisms of Evolution

The second important point that negates Darwin's theory is that both concepts put forward by the theory as "evolutionary mechanisms" were understood to have no evolutionary power in reality.

Darwin based his theory of evolution entirely on the mechanism of "natural selection". The importance he placed on this mechanism was evident in the name of his book: *The Origin of Species, By Means Of Natural Selection...*

Natural selection holds that those living things that are stronger and more suited to the natural conditions of their habitats will survive in the struggle for life. For example, in a deer herd under the threat of wild animals, those that can run faster will survive. Therefore, the deer herd will be comprised of faster and stronger individuals. However, unquestionably, this mechanism will not cause deer to evolve and transform them into another living species, for instance, horses.

Therefore, the mechanism of natural selection has no evolutionary power. Darwin was also aware of this fact and had to state this in his book *The Origin of Species* by saying: "Natural selection can do nothing until favourable variations chance to occur."[37]

Lamarck's Impact

So, how could these "favourable variations" occur? Darwin tried to answer this question from the standpoint of the primitive understanding of science in his age. According to the French biologist Lamarck, who lived before Darwin, living creatures passed the traits they acquired during their lifetime to the next generation and these traits, accumulating from one generation to another, caused new species to be formed. For instance, according to Lamarck, giraffes evolved from antelopes; as they struggled to eat the leaves of high trees, their necks were extended from generation to generation.

Darwin also gave similar examples, and in his book *The Origin of Species*, for instance, said that some bears going into water to find food transformed into whales over time.[38]

However, the laws of inheritance discovered by Mendel and verified by the science of genetics that flourished in the 20th century, utterly demolished the legend that acquired traits were passed on to subsequent generations. Thus, the theory of natural selection fell into disfavour as a factor in the story of evolution.

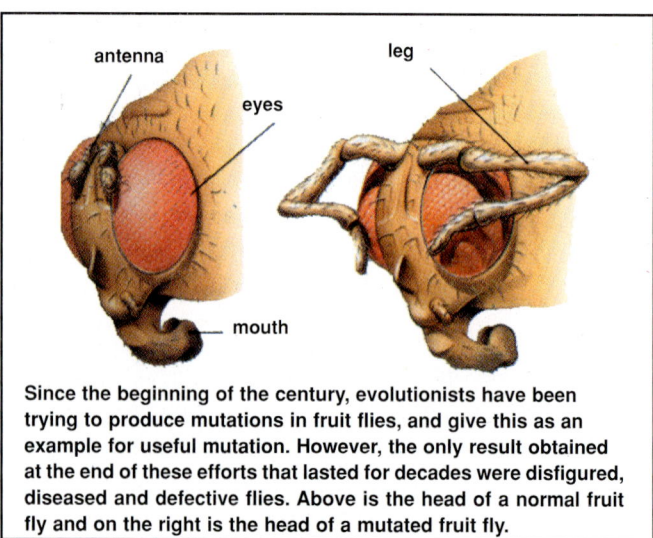

Since the beginning of the century, evolutionists have been trying to produce mutations in fruit flies, and give this as an example for useful mutation. However, the only result obtained at the end of these efforts that lasted for decades were disfigured, diseased and defective flies. Above is the head of a normal fruit fly and on the right is the head of a mutated fruit fly.

Neo-Darwinism and Mutations

In order to find a solution, Darwinists advanced the "Modern Synthetic Theory", or as it is more commonly known, Neo-Darwinism, at the end of the 1930's. To natural selection, Neo-Darwinism added mutations which are distortions formed in the genes of living beings because of external factors such as radiation or replication errors as the "cause of favourable variations."

Today, the model that stands for evolution in the world is Neo-Darwinism. The theory maintains that millions of living beings present on the earth formed as a result of a process whereby numerous complex organs of these organisms such as the ears, eyes, lungs, and wings, underwent "mutations," that is, genetic disorders. Yet, there is a clear cut scientific fact

The theory of evolution claims that living species gradually evolved from one another. The fossil record, however, explicitly falsifies this claim. For example, in the Cambrian Period, some 550 million years ago, tens of totally distinct living species emerged suddenly. These living beings depicted in the above picture have very complex structures. This fact, referred to as the "Cambrian Explosion" in scientific literature is plain evidence of creation.

that belies the theory. Mutations do not cause living beings to develop, but on the contrary, always cause them harm.

The reason for this is very simple: DNA has a very complex structure and random changes can only be damaging to it. American geneticist B.G. Ranganathan explains this as follows:

> Mutations are small, random, and harmful. They rarely occur and the best possibility is that they will be ineffectual. These four characteristics of mutations imply that mutations cannot lead to an evolutionary development. A random change in a highly specialised organism is either ineffectual or harmful. A random change in a watch cannot improve the watch. It will most probably harm it or at best be ineffectual. An earthquake does not improve the city, it brings destruction.[39]

Not surprisingly, no mutation example, which is useful, that is, which is observed to develop the genetic code, has been observed so far. All mutations have proved to be harmful. It was understood that mutation, which is presented as an "evolutionary mechanism," is actually a genetic occurrence that harms living beings, and leaves them disabled. (The most common effect of mutation on human beings is cancer). No doubt, a destructive mechanism cannot be an "evolutionary mechanism." Natural selection, on the other hand, "can do nothing by itself" as Darwin also accepted. This fact shows us that there is no "evolutionary mechanism" in nature. Since no evolutionary mechanism exists, neither could any imaginary process called evolution have taken place.

The Fossil Record: No Sign of Intermediate Forms

The clearest evidence that the scenario suggested by the theory of evolution did not take place is the fossil record.

According to the theory of evolution, every living species has sprung from a predecessor. A previously existing species turned into something else in time and all species have come into being in this way. According to the theory, this transformation proceeds gradually over millions of years.

Had this been the case, then numerous intermediary species should have existed and lived within this long transformation period.

The fossil record is a great barricade in front of the theory of evolution. The fossil record shows that living species emerged suddenly and fully-formed without any evolutionary transitional form between them. This fact is evidence that species are created separately.

For instance, some half-fish/half-reptiles should have lived in the past which had acquired some reptilian traits in addition to the fish traits they already had. Or there should have existed some reptile-birds, which acquired some bird traits in addition to the reptilian traits they already had. Since these would be in a transitional phase, they should be disabled, defective, crippled living beings. Evolutionists refer to these imaginary creatures, which they believe to have lived in the past, as "transitional forms."

If such animals had really existed, there should be millions and even billions of them in number and variety. More importantly, the remains of these strange creatures should be present in the fossil record. *In The Origin of Species*, Darwin explained:

> If my theory be true, numberless intermediate varieties, linking most closely all of the species of the same group together must assuredly have existed... Consequently, evidence of their former existence could be found only amongst fossil remains.[40]

Darwin's Hopes Shattered

However, although evolutionists have been conducting a vigorous search for fossils since the middle of the 19th century all over the world, no transitional forms have yet been uncovered. All the fossils unearthed in excavations showed that contrary to the expectations of evolutionists, life appeared on earth all of a sudden and fully-formed.

A famous British paleontologist, Derek V. Ager, admits this fact, even though he is an evolutionist:

> The point emerges that if we examine the fossil record in detail, whether at the level of orders or of species, we find—over and over again—not gradual evolution, but the sudden explosion of one group at the expense of another.[41]

This means that in the fossil record, all living species suddenly emerge as fully formed without any intermediate forms in between. This is just the opposite of Darwin's assumptions. Also, it is very strong evidence that living beings are created. The only explanation for a living species emerging suddenly and intact without any evolutionary ancestor would be that this species was created. This fact is admitted also by the widely known evolutionist biologist Douglas Futuyma:

> Creation and evolution, between them, exhaust the possible explanations for the origin of living things. Organisms either appeared on the earth fully developed or they did not. If they did not, they must have developed from pre-existing species by some process of modification. If they did appear in a fully developed state, they must indeed have been created by some omnipotent intelligence.[42]

Fossils show that living beings emerged completely and perfectly on the earth. That means that "the origin of species" is, contrary to Darwin's supposition, not evolution but creation.

The Tale of Human Evolution

The subject most often brought up by the advocates of the theory of evolution is that of the origin of man. The Darwinist claim holds that the

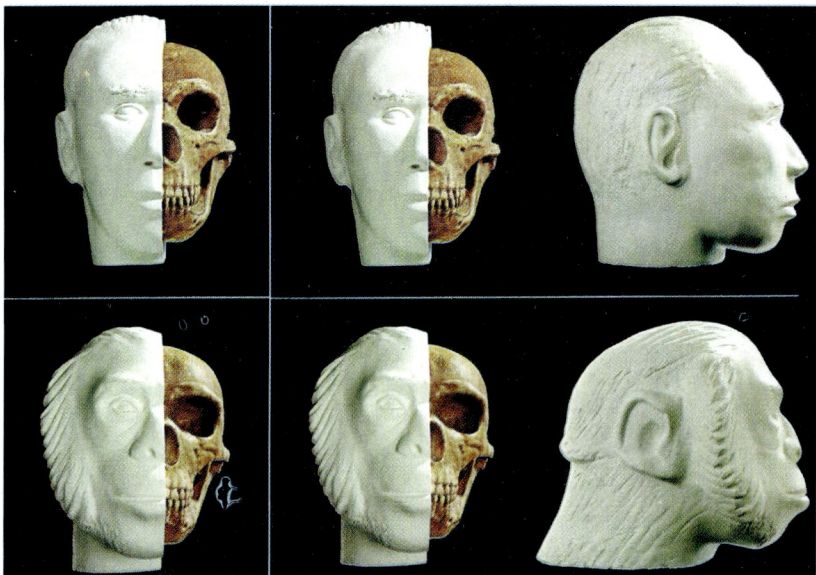

There are no fossil remains that support the tale of human evolution. On the contrary, the fossil record shows that there is an insurmountable barrier between apes and men. In the face of this truth, evolutionists fixed their hopes on certain drawings and models. They randomly place masks on the fossil remains and fabricate imaginary half-ape, half-human faces.

modern men of today evolved from some kind of ape-like creatures. During this alleged evolutionary process, which is supposed to have started 4-5 million years ago, it is claimed that there existed some "transitional forms" between modern man and his ancestors. According to this completely imaginary scenario, four basic "categories" are listed:

1. Australopithecus
2. Homo habilis
3. Homo erectus
4. Homo sapiens

Evolutionists call the so-called first ape-like ancestors of men "Australopithecus," which means "South African ape." These beings were actually nothing but an old ape species that became extinct. Extensive research done on various Australopithecus specimens by two world-renowned anatomists from England and the USA, namely, Lord Solly Zuckerman and Prof. Charles Oxnard, has shown that these belonged to an ordinary ape species that became extinct and bore no resemblance to humans.[43]

Evolutionists classify the next stage of human evolution as "homo," that is, "man". According to the evolutionist claim, the living beings in the Homo series are more developed than Australopithecus. Evolutionists make a fanciful evolution scheme by arranging different fossils of these creatures in a particular order. This scheme is imaginary, because it has never been proved that there is an evolutionary relation between these different classes. Ernst Mayr, one of the foremost defenders of the theory of evolution in the 20th century, admits this fact by saying that "the chain reaching as far as Homo sapiens is actually lost." [44]

By outlining the link chain as "Australopithecus > Homo habilis > Homo erectus > Homo sapiens," evolutionists imply that each of these species is another's ancestor. However, recent findings of paleoanthropologists have revealed that Australopithecus, Homo habilis and Homo erectus lived in different parts of the world in the same time.[45]

Moreover, a certain segment of humans classified as Homo erectus have lived up until very modern times. Homo sapiens neandarthalensis and Homo sapiens sapiens (modern man) co-existed in the same region.[46]

This situation apparently indicates the invalidity of the claim that any line of ancestry can be traced. A paleontologist from Harvard University, Stephen Jay Gould explains this deadlock in the theory of evolution, although he is an evolutionist himself:

> What has become of our ladder if there are three coexisting lineages of hominids (A. africanus, the robust australopithecines, and H. habilis), none clearly derived from another? Moreover, none of the three display any evolutionary trends during their tenure on earth.[47]

Put briefly, the scenario of human evolution, which is sought to be upheld with the help of various drawings of some "half ape, half human" creatures appearing in the media and course books, that is, by means of barefaced propaganda, is nothing but a tale with no scientific backing.

Lord Solly Zuckerman, one of the most famous and respected scientists in the U.K., who carried out research on this subject for years, and particularly studied Australopithecus fossils for 15 years, finally concluded, despite being an evolutionist himself, that there is in reality no such family tree branching out from ape-like creatures to man.

Zuckerman also made an interesting "spectrum of science." He formed a spectrum of sciences ranging from those he considered scientific to those he considered unscientific. According to Zuckerman's spectrum, the most "scientific"—that is, depending on concrete data—fields of science are chemistry and physics. After them come the biological sciences and then the social sciences. At the far end of the spectrum, which is the part considered to be most "unscientific," are extra-sensory perception–including telepathy and the "sixth sense"–and finally "human evolution." Zuckerman explains his reasoning:

> We then move right off the register of objective truth into those fields of presumed biological science, like extrasensory perception or the interpretation of man's fossil history, where to the faithful (evolutionist) anything is possible - and where the ardent believer (in evolution) is sometimes able to believe several contradictory things at the same time.[48]

The tale of human evolution adds up to little more than the prejudiced interpretations of a number of fossils unearthed by certain people, who blindly adhere to their theory.

Technology In The Eye and The Ear

Another subject that remains unanswered by evolutionary theory is the excellent quality of perception in the eye and the ear.

Before passing on to the subject of the eye, let us briefly answer the question of "how we see". Light rays coming from an object fall oppositely on the retina of the eye. Here, these light rays are transmitted into electric signals by cells and they reach a tiny spot at the back of the brain called the centre of vision. These electric signals are perceived in this centre of the brain as an image after a series of processes. With this technical background, let us do some thinking.

The brain is insulated from light. That means that the inside of the brain is solid dark, and light does not reach the location where the brain is situated. The place called the centre of vision is a solid dark place where no light ever reaches; it may even be the darkest place you have ever known. However, you observe a luminous, bright world in this pitch darkness.

The image formed in the eye is so sharp and distinct that even the technology of the 20th century has not been able to attain it. For instance, look at the book you read, your hands with which you hold it, then lift your head and look around you. Have you ever seen such a sharp and distinct image as this one at any other place? Even the most developed television screen produced by the greatest television producer in the world cannot provide such a sharp image for you. This is a three-dimensional, coloured, and extremely sharp image. For more than 100 years, thousands of engineers have been trying to achieve this sharpness. Factories, huge premises were established, much research has been done, plans and designs have been made for this purpose. Again, look at a TV screen and the book you hold in your hands. You will see that there is a big difference in sharpness and distinction. Moreover, the TV screen shows you a two-dimensional image, whereas with your eyes, you watch a three-dimensional perspective having depth.

For many years, ten of thousands of engineers have tried to make a three-dimensional TV, and reach the vision quality of the eye. Yes, they have made a three-dimensional television system but it is not possible to watch it without putting on glasses; moreover, it is only an artificial three-dimension. The background is more blurred, the foreground appears like a paper setting. Never has it been possible to produce a sharp and distinct vision like that of the eye. In both the camera and the television, there is a loss of image quality.

Evolutionists claim that the mechanism producing this sharp and distinct image has been formed by chance. Now, if somebody told you that the television in your room was formed as a result of chance, that all its atoms just happened to come together and make up this device that produces an image, what would you think? How can atoms do what thousands of people cannot?

If a device producing a more primitive image than the eye could not have been formed by chance, then it is very evident that the eye and the image seen by the eye could not have been formed by chance. The same situation applies to the ear. The outer ear picks up the available sounds by the auricle and directs them to the middle ear; the middle ear transmits the sound vibrations by intensifying them; the inner ear sends these vibrations to the brain by translating them into electric signals. Just as with the eye, the act of hearing finalises in the centre of hearing in the brain.

The situation in the eye is also true for the ear. That is, the brain is insulated from sound just like it is from light: it does not let any sound in. Therefore, no matter how noisy is the outside, the inside of the brain is completely silent. Nevertheless, the sharpest sounds are perceived in the brain. In your brain, which is insulated from sound, you listen to the symphonies of an orchestra, and hear all the noises in a crowded place. However, if the sound level in your brain was measured by a precise device at that moment, it would be seen that a complete silence is prevailing there.

As is the case with imagery, decades of effort have been spent in trying to generate and reproduce sound that is faithful to the original. The results of these efforts are sound recorders, high-fidelity systems, and systems for sensing sound. Despite all this technology and the thousands of engineers and experts who have been working on this endeavour, no sound has yet been obtained that has the same sharpness and clarity as the sound perceived by the ear. Think of the highest-quality HI-FI systems produced by the biggest company in the music industry. Even in these devices, when sound is recorded some of it is lost; or when you turn on a HI-FI you always hear a hissing sound before the music starts. However, the sounds that are the products of the technology of the human body are extremely sharp and clear. A human ear never perceives a sound accompanied by a hissing sound or with atmospherics as does HI-FI; it perceives sound exactly as it is, sharp and clear. This is the way it has been since the creation of man.

So far, no visual or recording apparatus produced by man has been as sensitive and successful in perceiving sensory data as are the eye and the ear.

However, as far as seeing and hearing are concerned, a far greater fact lies beyond all this.

To Whom Does the Consciousness that Sees and Hears Within the Brain Belong?

Who is it that watches an alluring world in its brain, listens to symphonies and the twittering of birds, and smells the rose?

The stimulations coming from the eyes, ears, and nose of a human being travel to the brain as electro-chemical nervous impulses. In biology, physiology, and biochemistry books, you can find many details about how this image forms in the brain. However, you will never come across the most important fact about this subject: Who is it that perceives these electro-chemical nervous impulses as images, sounds, odours and sensory events in the brain? There is a consciousness in the brain that perceives all this without feeling any need for eye, ear, and nose. To whom does this consciousness belong? There is no doubt that this consciousness does not belong to the nerves, the fat layer and neurons comprising the brain. This is why Darwinist-materialists, who believe that everything is comprised of matter, cannot give any answer to these questions.

For this consciousness is the spirit created by God. The spirit needs neither the eye to watch the images, nor the ear to hear the sounds. Furthermore, nor does it need the brain to think.

Everyone who reads this explicit and scientific fact should ponder on Almighty God, should fear Him and seek refuge in Him, He Who squeezes the entire universe in a pitch-dark place of a few cubic centimeters in a three-dimensional, coloured, shadowy, and luminous form.

A Materialist Faith

The information we have presented so far shows us that the theory of evolution is a claim evidently at variance with scientific findings. The theory's claim about the origin of life is inconsistent with science, the evolutionary mechanisms it proposes have no evolutionary power, and the fossil record demonstrates that the intermediate forms required by the theory never existed. So, it certainly follows that the theory of evolution should be set aside as an unscientific idea. This is how many ideas, such as the earth-centered universe model, have been removed from the agenda of science throughout history.

However, the theory of evolution is insistently kept on the agenda of science. Certain individuals even try to present criticisms directed against the theory as an "attack on science." Why?

The reason is that the theory of evolution is an indispensable dogmatic belief for some circles. These circles are blindly devoted to materialist philosophy and adopt Darwinism because it is the only materialist explanation that can be put forward for nature.

Interestingly enough, they also admit to this fact from time to time. A well-known geneticist and an outspoken evolutionist, Richard C. Lewontin from Harvard University, confesses that he is "foremost a materialist and then a scientist" with these words:

It is not that the methods and institutions of science somehow compel us to accept a material explanation of the phenomenal world, but, on the contrary, that we are forced by our a priori adherence to material causes to create an apparatus of investigation and a set of concepts that produce material explanations, no matter how counter-intuitive, no matter how mystifying to the uninitiated. Moreover, that materialism is absolute, so we cannot allow a Divine Foot in the door.[49]

These are explicit statements that Darwinism is a dogma kept alive just for the sake of adherence to the materialist philosophy. This dogma maintains that there is no being save matter. Therefore, it argues that inanimate, unconscious matter created life. It suggests that millions of different living species, for instance, birds, fish, giraffes, tigers, insects, trees, flowers, whales and human beings originated as a result of the interactions between matter, such as the pouring rain, the lightning flash, etc., i.e. out of inanimate matter. This is a precept contrary both to reason and science. Yet Darwinists continue to defend this precept in order "not to allow a Divine Foot in the door."

Anyone who does not look at the origin of living beings with a materialist prejudice will see this evident truth: All living beings are works of a Creator, Who is All-Powerful, All-Wise and All-Knowing. This Creator is God, Who created the whole universe from non-existence, designed it in the most perfect form, and fashioned all living beings.

They said: "Glory be to You!
We have no knowledge except what You have
taught us. You are the All-Knowing, the All-Wise."
(Surat al-Baqarah: 32)

NOTES

1. Orhan Hançerlioğlu, *Düşünce Tarihi* (History of Idea), Remzi Kitabevi, İstanbul: 1987, p.432

2. Orhan Hançerlioğlu, *Düşünce Tarihi* (History of Idea), Remzi Kitabevi, İstanbul: 1987, p.447

3. Frederick Vester, *Denken, Lernen, Vergessen, vga, 1978,* p. 6

4. George Politzer, *Principes Fondamentaux de Philosophie,* Editions Sociales, Paris, 1954, pp. 38-39-44

5. *Bilim ve Teknik* Magazine (Science and Technology), No. 227, p. 6-7

6. R.L.Gregory, *Eye and Brain*: The Psychology of Seeing, Oxford University Press Inc. New York, 1990, p.9

7. George Berkeley, *A Treatise Concerning the Principles of Human Knowledge",* 1710, Works of George Berkeley, vol. I, ed. A. Fraser, Oxford, 1871

8. Lincoln Barnett, *The Universe and Dr. Einstein,* William Sloane Associate, New York, 1948, p. 20

9. Bertrand Russell, *ABC of Relativity,* George Allen and Unwin, London, 1964, pp. 161-162

10. George Berkeley, *A Treatise Concerning the Principles of Human Knowledge",* 1710, Works of George Berkeley, vol. I, ed. A. Fraser, Oxford, 1871 p. 35-36

11. Ali Demirsoy, *Kalıtım ve Evrim* (Inheritance and Evolution), p.4

12. Bertrand Russell, *What is the Soul?,* Works of George Berkeley, vol. I, ed. A. Fraser, Oxford, 1871

13. Bertrand Russell, *Three Dialogues Between Hylas and Philonous,* Works of George Berkeley, vol. I, ed. A. Fraser, Oxford, 1871

14. George Politzer, *Principes Fondamentaux de Philosophie,* Editions Sociales, Paris, 1954, p. 40

15. *Bilim ve Teknik* Magazine (Science and Technology), No:111, p.2

16. R.L.Gregory, *Eye and Brain: The Psychology of Seeing,* Oxford University Press Inc. New York, 1990, p.9

17. Ken Wilber, *Holographic Paradigm and Other Paradoxes,* p.20

18. Bertrand Russell, *ABC of Relativity,* George Allen and Unwin, London, 1964, pp. 161-162

19. Henri Bergson, *Matter and Memory,* Zone Books, New York, 1991

20. David Hume, *A Treatise of Human Nature,* Book I, Section IV: Of Personal Identity

21. İmam Rabbani, *Hz. Mektupları* (Letters of Rabbani), Vol II, 357. Letter, p. 163

22. İmam Rabbani, *Hz. Mektupları* (Letters of Rabbani), Vol II, 470. Letter, p.1432

23. François Jacob, *Le Jeu Des Possibles,* University of Washington Press, 1982, p. 111

24. Lincoln Barnett, *The Universe and Dr.*